The Diamonds of Dixie

The Diamonds of Dixie

Travels through the Southern Minor Leagues

ERNEST J. GREEN

Madison Books

LANHAM • NEW YORK • LONDON

Published by Madison Books
4720 Boston Way
Lanham, Maryland 20706

12 Hid's Copse Road
Cumnor Hill, Oxford OX2 9JJ, England

Distributed by National Book Network

Library of Congress Cataloging-in-Publication Data

Green, Ernest J.
    The diamonds of Dixie : travels through the southern minor leagues / Ernest
J. Green
        p.   cm.
    Includes index.
        ISBN 1-56833-043-X (cloth : alk. paper) — ISBN 1-56833-111-8 (pbk. :
alk. paper)
        1. Minor league baseball—Southern States.   I. Title.
    GV875.A1G73   1995
    796.357'64'0975—dc20   94-39409

ISBN 1-56833-043-X (cloth : alk. paper)
ISBN 1-56833-111-8 (pbk. : alk. paper)

♾ᵀᴹ The paper used in this publication meets the minimum requirements of
American National Standard for Information Sciences—Permanence of
Paper for Printed Library Materials, ANSI Z39.48–1984.
Manufactured in the United States of America.

Dedicated with love
to my wife
Zena
who took me back
after my summer romance
with baseball

I tell you something else and you can mark this down as a prediction. You give this country twenty or thirty more years, everybody's got any sense is going down South.

SATCHEL PAIGE

Contents

Acknowledgments

FOR MORE THAN A QUARTER CENTURY I was lucky enough to have colleagues who shared a fondness for the national pastime: the late Righton Robertson, Harold Guy, Sherman Silverman, Bruce Dudley, my frequent companion to baseball games and a historian who wrote *Distant Drums*, about the 1948 Cleveland Indians, Dennis Sullivan, with his encyclopedic command of baseball data, and Bob Coords. Our offices were all located on the same corridor within a distance about equal to that from home plate to second base (that's 127 feet, $3^3/_8$ inches, for the uninitiated), and if I stepped into the hall and dropped a comment on the latest trade or the current standings, I soon collected a small crowd of these folk. Over the years they all helped to sustain my affection for the game and made me a more informed student of it.

David Lamb was generous in sharing his experiences of baseball travel and provided many useful suggestions. Cathy Burns contributed helpful trip analysis and helped me keep my goals in sight.

I visited thirty southern baseball clubs during the 1993 season. My thanks go to all the players, general managers, field managers, and other club officials who took time to talk with me during the visits, which lasted up to seven days. I invariably showed up at the worst time of day in the midst of a busy home stand, and they were gracious and cooperative.

My wife, Zena, is a lukewarm baseball fan at best. At her most enthusiastic, she says that it is nice to sit in the sunshine or in the cool evening air on a pleasant June night. Yet she has been my companion at more games than anyone else over the years, and her company has been appreciated all the more because it reflects a bond that baseball didn't have to forge.

My sons Michael and Laurence unfortunately inherited more of their mother's baseball genes than mine, but I can usually coax them into going with me to one game a year each. They both encouraged my trip; neither of them ever said there was anything peculiar about having a father who drove away a summer going to minor league baseball games.

I appreciate the extra effort put forth by Julie Kirsch and the other production staff at Madison Books to make the book materialize by Opening Day. And if editors were diamonds, Jennifer Ruark and Jon Sisk would be several carats each. They saw a book in the pages I gave them; then had the skill and patience to help me see it too.

Others to whom I owe thanks for information, assistance or support are mentioned in the text. In a few cases, I have, as promised, provided pseudonyms for protection of privacy.

Introduction:
Seeds of a Summer Odyssey

MANY BOOKS HAVE BEEN WRITTEN about baseball, and many more about the South. Until now, no one book has specifically wed these two subjects. They were, for awhile, reluctant marriage partners anyway. In the nineteenth century, baseball was mainly a north-eastern sport spreading toward the Midwest, not the South. Its early icons and images reflected this geography: Cooperstown, New York; Elysian Fields, Hoboken, New Jersey; the great 1869 Cincin-nati Red Stockings. When baseball did spread to the South, it was minor league baseball, not the big-time stuff. Until recently, south-ern baseball meant the Southern Association, the Texas League, and the even smaller leagues and their backwater towns. Baseball has been played in the South for a long time, nevertheless, played well and played badly just as in other parts of the country. I once sat next to a fan at a minor league game in Alabama, a beefy square-faced man who stuffed tobacco from a Red Man pouch into his jaw without looking at the pouch, the tobacco, or his hand.

"How do you think baseball is different in the South than in other parts of the country?" I asked him in my best interviewer manner.

He narrowed his eyes in deep thought. "The players sweat more," he replied finally, slowly letting loose with a large, satisfied grin.

The poet Donald Hall seconds his sentiment: "Baseball is a

Inside, distances to the fences were 330 feet down each line and 390 feet to center field. A covered grandstand, supported by wooden beams, ran from behind home plate a short way past first and third, and a wooden press box sat on the roof. In left field, bleachers had been erected above the fence for the Knot Hole Gang, where young fans could see games for a dime. My friend John J. Kidd and I were too advanced at ages twelve and up to sit in the Knot Hole section, and proudly paid our thirty-five cents to sit with the adults in the bleachers.

Enclosing the vast green carpet of grass, colorful outfield fences advertised Tulsa commercial institutions: Froug's Department Stores, Meadow Gold Milk, the Golden Drumstick Restaurant. The entrance to the tunnel leading to the Oiler's clubhouse adjoined the corner of the right field bleachers and John J. and I hung around there, hoping to pick up a few bits of wisdom from the players.

We saw gritty second baseman Johnny Temple play two seasons for Tulsa in 1951 and 1952 before moving up to the National League. Johnny was a four-time National League all-star for the Reds and made history by being part of the first interleague trade. On December 15, 1959, he was dealt to Cleveland and three players (one of whom was Billy Martin) came to the Reds. We saw Johnny Vander Meer, famous for his double no-hitter with Cincinnati years earlier, play out his career with Tulsa in 1952. He looked ancient to us, and in fact was by baseball standards, but put together a commendable season, going 11–10 with a 2.30 ERA. More notably, he threw his third no-hitter in professional baseball that season, beating Shreveport 12–0. In 1953, Nino Escalera thrilled us by hitting nineteen triples and by sliding into first base on every close play. Given a long look by Cincinnati in 1954, he couldn't hit big-league pitching but he could run and run and run.

Minor league rosters had more stability in the 1950s than they do today. One of my favorite players was Fletcher Robbe, who played with Tulsa from 1950 through 1952. He never made it to the big leagues and didn't exactly set the Texas League on fire, but as the right fielder he was the player nearest to where we always sat and would sometimes say a few words to us between innings.

Every home game, before the bottom of the first, a shrill-voiced

Tulsa supporter would get on the PA system and roar out the Oiler rallying cry, "Lets goooooooooooooooooooooooooo Tulsa!" His name was Andy Andrews and he became a local institution. By the early 1950s, Andy the fan had become an Oiler employee, and listening to his call, we assumed that Tulsa ball games would forever begin with that booming voice bouncing around the park like an echo.

Attendance at Oiler games in the early 1950s was usually four or five hundred, modest by today's standards but impressive to a boy growing up in Collinsville, Oklahoma (population one thousand). Crowds would swell to five or six thousand for the Texas League play-offs, and all around town people would talk about whether Tulsa would make it to the Dixie Series with the Southern Association winner. Championships were always celebrated with downtown parades and were widely reported in newspapers and on the radio.

Lonnie Kidd, John J.'s father, was a frenzied fan who brooked no flaws in Oiler players, and would often have to calm himself by wringing his hands and stomping up and down the bleacher seats after "another boneheaded play." Even in the pickup bed we could hear him on the way home after a loss, cursing and bemoaning Oiler frailties, bad officiating, and devious tricks by the opposition. The game didn't end when Lonnie left Texas League Park on those warm summer evenings in Tulsa.

The same summer I began attending Tulsa Oilers' games, I made a two-week long trip across the South with my father and grandfather. We visited relatives in Tennessee, Georgia, and northern Florida; it was the first time I had left Oklahoma. I saw Spanish moss, watched families leave early in the mornings to pick cotton, and swam in the dark, tepid rivers of the Florida panhandle. I came home carrying an exotic vision of the Deep South in my mind, a wondrous, mystical set of images that endure still today. I learned separately about professional baseball and the South during my twelfth summer, but they became twirled around each other like the softly spun layers of cotton candy sold at concession stands in Texas League Park.

My love affair with baseball has been intense and passionate at times, but it has never been the constant, dogged devotion I have seen in others. Twice I have broken up with the old game, told her to go away, that I didn't want to see her any more. The first time was in the late 1960s, when, for a time, the game lost its traditional balance as pitchers began to dominate. Then Oklahoma idol Mickey Mantle retired in 1968, and as a final straw, the Washington Senators left my adopted city in 1971, moving, ironically, to a new location between the old Texas League towns of Fort Worth and Dallas. The breakup lasted for a few years, and then like a reformed lover, I began to call again. After we made up, I behaved myself as a fan for awhile. The second divorce was in the late 1980s. Lockouts, salary disputes, monetary concerns, and scandals were then taking precedence over the game itself in the media. Who needs you? I said. My attendance at the nearest major league ballpark, Memorial Stadium in Baltimore, dropped from twenty or thirty games a year to only two or three.

Addictions aren't that easy to cure, however. In 1989 a Carolina League team moved to Frederick, Maryland, an easy drive from where I live. I went to one game in Frederick that year, a late season spur-of-the-moment trip I had somehow talked my wife into making, and arrived to find that the game was sold out. A business organization had bought all the tickets and had given away coupons locally for game admission. The ticket offices weren't even open. We walked up to the gate to find out what was going on.

Yes, it was sold out, the gatekeeper said. He asked how far we had come, decided that it was too far to drive and not see a baseball game, and let us in anyway.

I may not have known it at that exact moment, but the love affair was back on; baseball and I were an item once more. Frederick is a handsome little city, sheltered by the low-slung Catoctin Mountains to the west. Clean, with a busy historic district and good restaurants, the town was once described by John Greenleaf Whittier in his poem *Barbara Fritchie:*

> The clustered spires of Frederick stand
> 'neath the green-walled hills of Maryland

In other words, a perfect town for a ballpark. In 1990, the Frederick Keys—named for famous son Francis Scott Key, author of the *Star Spangled Banner*—opened a new park, Harry Grove Stadium. I went often that year, sometimes with others, sometimes stopping by the park alone after a day of fishing the clear trout streams of the Catoctins to the north and west. I was getting reacquainted with minor league baseball, after forsaking it for almost thirty years in favor of the big-time version. During one game that year, as it began to rain, ushers, front office people (including a woman in a skirt and hosiery), concession stand attendants, and even a half dozen fans splashed onto the field and rather ineffectually began to unroll the tarp. Several fell, got up laughing, and walked off the field looking limp and damp. That year attendance soared, fueled by the fact that the Keys had a good ball team.

Zena and I were present at the concluding game of the Carolina League play-offs in September. The Keys were tied with the Kinston Indians, two games apiece. In the final game, Kinston took an early 5–0 lead and still led 5–3 when the Keys mounted a rally in the sixth. With runners on first and second, the public address announcer said the two short words that were the team's rallying call: "Shake 'em!" Cheering and other noises stopped as thousands of fans removed key chains from pockets and purses and in unison, began to gently jangle them, building a melodic, haunting noise like the sounds of a thousand wind chimes at a yoga *ashram*. Tim Holland, whose name will never become a household word among major league fans, hit one over the left field wall, over the three tiers of colorful billboards, out into the night and the Keys held on to win the league championship. Instead of retreating to the clubhouse to celebrate, team officials hustled champagne onto the infield after the last out. As Kinston's defeated Indians slunk toward their team bus, the Keys began tackling each other on the infield grass, spraying champagne wildly, and after soaking themselves, coaches, and others on the field, ran over and began spraying fans who were clustered close enough to the seat rails to be within firing range.

Baseball fans everywhere know that you have to sit through a batch of routine, ultimately meaningless and anticlimactic games to sift out the one where drama, purpose, and well-timed heroics provide a memorable experience. A few even know that this trade-off is not only inevitable, but worth it. This was the one.

Around that time, a plan began to form in my mind. I had been teaching sociology at a college in Maryland for what would amount to twenty-seven years in 1993. At age fifty-four, exactly half my life had been spent in one job. I applied for a study leave for 1993 and at first intended to use it to go out and experience life, then return to teach with more authenticity, to leave familiar environs and return with more to say than when I left. I intended to head south when the baseball season opened, and to follow the region's minor leagues across the South until the South ceased to exist. I arranged a leave, concluded my preliminary research, and readied my transportation. Then, only about two weeks before the scheduled departure, I realized that I wouldn't be returning to the college. As Thoreau said when he left Walden Pond after being there two years, two months, and six days, I couldn't spare any more time for that particular life. I told the necessary people of my intentions, and although technically still on the payroll while on the trip, mentally I had become a free agent; cut loose, unhired, retired; my tenure had expired. The only work I would have when I returned would be whatever I brought with me from the trip. My realization that I had other lives to live had taken me a quarter century longer than Thoreau's, but it was no more revocable.

By late winter two central questions were becoming fixed in my mind. Was the traditional South with its distinctive subculture still down there, or had the second half of the twentieth century homogenized it? I believed the Old South of my youthful memories was alive somewhere, pulled back from the interstates, hiding behind a forest of television antennas and satellite dishes, and that I could find it. Was minor league baseball still an important southern institution, or had the major league penetration into Florida, Georgia, and Texas eclipsed the region's enthusiasm for local teams? I thought, and hoped, that modern day Lonnie Kidds still left the southern ballparks with the devout ravings I had heard in the back of that old bricklayer's pickup.

Questions formed, plans made, gas tank full, I spent February and March the way baseball fans always spend those months: waiting for Opening Day.

1

Quiet Nights in the Sunshine State

IMPATIENCE LANDED ME IN FLORIDA while opening day for the minor leagues was still a day away. I stopped in Miami Beach for some sight-seeing, and I spent several hours examining the architecture in the art deco district. I have driven fifty miles out of my way to see one art deco structure, so the allure of an entire neighborhood of these flashy, wildly colored structures was irresistible. The district's one square mile contains over four hundred buildings, almost all built in the 1930s during the heyday of art deco construction. Hotels of Miami Beach have all the usual features of the streamline moderne version of art deco, plus vibrant tropical colors. As they took their livelihood from proximity to the ocean, architects added nautical references like porthole windows and balconies reminiscent of decks on a luxury liner.

When I returned to my truck, parked in front of a curved and blocked hotel painted a brilliant yellow and white, I was struck by how well the vehicle blended into the city's aesthetic. My transportation for the trip was a full-sized 1972 Chevrolet pickup, bought new by my stepfather in that long ago year when the country re-elected Richard Nixon and the Vietnam War continued to cut our society into rancorous fragments. I had become its owner just three years previously, after my stepfather's death, and had driven the truck little. Its bright white and two-tone olive paint remained shiny, and it was a fine piece of machinery. Although it had been state of the art twenty-one years ago, nothing on the inside was LED or LCD. Needles fluttered and pointed at numbers, light bulbs

1

moment. In fact, another serious storm had come through the area since Andrew, further setting back the cleanup.

Even seven months after Andrew, a sense of disorientation prevailed. Natural disasters not only wreak physical havoc, but also alter people's psychological maps. Landmarks disappear, neighbors leave, boundaries become vague, gone are neighborhood gateways and the sense of security one feels when entering a familiar place. The men worked mechanically and without humor. The people of Homestead would need many seasons before the effects of Andrew no longer dominated their lives.

A week after I passed through Homestead, the community received another serious blow. The Cleveland Indians canceled prehurricane plans to build a spring training complex in Homestead. They reasoned that the area could not be expected to recover economically, and now it would not receive the millions of dollars from construction, continuing jobs, and increased tourism that would have accrued if the Indians had followed through on their plans. Homestead was becoming the victim of a self-fulfilling prophecy. Investors were deciding that the area could not become economically viable again, and by their actions were assuring that this prediction would become true.

I intended to begin the minor league baseball season on the west coast of Florida, so I picked up US 41, the Tamiami Trail, at the junction with Florida 997. Before crossing, I stopped for gas and when I returned from paying, found an elderly gentleman eyeing the back of Sweetspot.

"Oughtn't to keep a dog in the back there on a day like this. Heat'll kill him."

Taking a cue from David Lamb, an earlier baseball traveler, I had placed a BEWARE OF DOG sign on the back camper window in hopes of discouraging anyone from trying to enter. No one was paying any attention to us, so I said, "I don't really have a dog. Just the sign."

"You ain't got no dog in there?"

"No. I just put the sign up so people would think there was a dog."

"You got a dog at home?"

4

"No. I have a cat. Her name is Fingers." This, I realized as soon as it was out, was unnecessary, and served to confuse the man more.

"I hope you ain't got no dog in there. Heat'll kill him if you do."

It was hot, around ninety degrees, but the screened windows were open and the white top reflected the heat. I started to explain this, then remembered that the dog was a fiction anyway, and just got in the pickup. Many people asked about the dog during the three-month trip. I usually found it simpler to lie when they asked what kind of dog I had, especially if it was someone who I knew wouldn't ask to see it. The breed became more ferocious each time I told the lie, and the lie became easier and easier to tell.

Driving across the Everglades, I saw people fishing in the canal that runs next to the Tamaimi Trail for much of its length. Almost all of the black people who were fishing sat on the bank and used long cane poles, their corks bobbing in the middle of the watercourse. The white fishermen were too sophisticated for such equipment. They took boats out into the narrow canal, and cast back toward the bank with fancy spinning reels and fiberglass rods, fishing exactly the same water reachable with the cane poles.

The Florida State League is a class A minor league, and is the only baseball coalition in which all the teams belong to cities in the same state. Historically, the circuit goes back to 1919 when it was formed as a class D league, and with only the depression years 1929 through 1935 missing, it existed through 1941 at either the class C or D level. The league reformed after the war, and the present setup has been in place since 1946. Under the classification restructuring of 1962, all class B, C, and D leagues were designated class A, where the Florida State League continues. The league is considered by baseball people to be advanced A, and jumps from the Florida State even to the majors are not unknown.

As a setting for player development, the league enjoys many advantages. Not much travel is necessary because the teams reside so close to each other, and an east-west divisional structure makes for even shorter travel time and distances. Most of the teams occupy major league spring training facilities, so their clubhouses, playing fields, and training equipment are superior to class A teams in other leagues. The weather is good even in spring, so few dates are canceled because of rain. The league is a bonus for major league affiliates, who would have to maintain the facilities for spring training anyway.

As community institutions, however, teams of the Florida State League have many shortcomings. The baseball parks are modern but generally synthetic, symmetrical, and without character. Attendance is by far the worst of any advanced A league in baseball. (In 1992 the average attendance for the eleven clubs that fielded teams in 1993 was 86,667. This compared to an average club attendance of 126,240 in the California League and 187,255 in the Carolina League. By the middle of the Miami Marlins' first season in 1993, the big league presence in Florida had helped drop the minor league turnstile count by 100,000.)

Attendance figures can be misleading because clubs give away tickets or sell them at tremendous discounts to sponsors. The Florida State clubs I visited gave away tickets with the best of them. A fan in Port Charlotte went through the list of season promotions and showed me how it was possible to obtain free or reduced-price tickets for most home dates. Even with giveaways, five Florida State franchises had total season attendance figures lower than one 1993 home game of the new Colorado Rockies when they topped eighty thousand fans.

One problem with Florida State League attendance, as former major leaguer Wally Moon pointed out to me later in the trip, is that the fields were set up for major league players. Average fence distances for the parks in 1993 were left—335 feet, center—406 feet, and right—332 feet. More importantly, power alleys of 380 to 390 feet were common. Fans who go to the park to see home runs leave disappointed often in Florida.

The most important reason for lack of fan support, however, is that Florida has fewer of the traditional communities that exist in the rest of the country. Most people are from somewhere else and have little identification with the area aside from the condominium or housing complex in which they live. In other parts of the country, parents take children to games; here, the elderly are separated from families and if they have any allegiance to a baseball team, it is "up north." Even the names of some towns sound like meaningless creations of real estate developers rather than references to the community's history.

Whether cause or effect of low attendance, most of the Florida minor league teams do little to promote community identification with the local club. At Charlotte County Stadium, home of the Charlotte Rangers, I picked up a copy of the program and the first several pages contained feature articles on officials of the parent club, the Texas Rangers. The parent organizations own most of the Florida State teams, an unusual situation throughout minor league baseball. With the exception of the Fort Meyer Miracle, every other club in the league has taken the name of the major league club. But the name Rangers, which means something in Texas because of the historical connection with the Texas Rangers of the nineteenth century, has no significance in Port Charlotte, Florida. Many Florida teams even wear the uniform colors of their big league counterparts.

Charlotte County Stadium is suburban and county oriented rather than community based. The architecture is postmodern, with a cantilevered grandstand roof so small that it provides fans with almost no protection from sun or rain. Charlotte's diamond is its most redeeming feature: beautiful dark green grass with checkerboard cuts in the infield and outfield, and with striking diagonal lines coursing through the grass along the foul lines. Tom Burns, the head groundskeeper, has won well-deserved awards for the immaculately tailored field. Walking up the ramp to a first vision of the field, green and brown with colorfully painted signs as a backdrop and with earthy smells radiating from the plush grass and moistened dirt, a fan could almost forgive the other departures from tradition. The results of the game, a rather lackluster affair in which players from both teams freely displayed evidence of early season rustiness, appeared in neither the Fort Meyer nor the Port Charlotte papers the following day. All I could find were the final Florida State League scores; even box scores were absent.

After the game I drove back to a campground on an island off Fort Meyers Beach. The campsites were just across the dunes from the Gulf of Mexico and the whisper of the surf drifted through swales in the mounds of sand. Pines sheltered the campsites and grew to the inland edge of the dunes. Playing against the sound of the surf, wind whistled softly through the pine needles. Henry Beston, who spent a year living in the isolation of a small shack on a remote part of Cape Cod in the 1920s, set down an account of his life there in *The Outermost House*. He wrote: "The three great elemental sounds in nature are the sound of rain, the sound of wind in a primeval wood, and the sound of outer ocean on a beach." About three o'clock in the morning, I awakened. The wind, coming out of the west, was blowing harder, bending the pines and kicking up the surf more forcefully. As I listened, rain began to pelt Sweetspot's camper roof and, for the only time in my life, I heard all three sounds at once.

The next evening in Sarasota produced a baseball experience much like the one the evening before in Port Charlotte. The stadium, Ed Smith, at least has a name instead of a geopolitical location for a title. Sarasota, a Chicago White Sox farm club, started major league right-hander Dave Stieb. He was on the major league fifteen-day disabled list and had come down to get in shape before rejoining Chicago. Despite the attraction of a major league pitcher, only a few hundred fans were in the stadium. Stieb was probably just as happy that there weren't more fans, since he gave up four runs in the first inning, two on home runs.

I sat behind home plate next to a boy of about twelve or thirteen, one of three alternating batboys Sarasota employed for home games. We began talking about the duties of a batboy—putting out water bottles, picking up bats and other equipment, taking balls to the umpire—and I made a few notes.

"Am I being interviewed?" he asked.

"I thought we were just talking."

His face fell.

"Okay, you got me. I was trying to be cagey about it but you're being interviewed."

He brightened. He told me that his name was Steve Dubois. When I asked him to spell it, he said "S-T-E-V-E."

Steve worked two of every three home games, one each for the home and visiting teams. The third night, which was this night, was his night off. He made five dollars per game plus fringe benefits.

"Which are?" I asked.

"We get to shag flies during batting practice and they give us some of the cracked bats to keep."

At his age, I would have offered to pay the club five dollars a game for a job like that.

On my other side sat a delightful Irish family, the McClory's, who were on vacation in Sarasota and attending their first ever baseball game. Growing up in the United States, even nonbaseball fans absorb some of the language and a general sense of the game. In Ireland, however, there is no such cultural anchorage. I tried to explain the essentials of the game.

"The catcher is signaling the pitcher now for the location and type of pitch he wants, and the batter isn't supposed to look around at the signal."

"The batter would be the chap who wants to strike the ball?" asked Ashley McClory, age fourteen.

The following day was clear and bright. I drove up to St. Petersburg to visit the offices of the National Association of Professional Baseball Leagues, which is the administrative head and governing body of minor league baseball, and the counterpart to major league baseball. Currently there are over two hundred baseball clubs and nineteen leagues in the association. Each league has its own president and officers, and league affairs are managed by these executives under their league bylaws, the National Association Agreement, and the Professional Baseball Agreement (commonly referred to as the PBA), which covers the relationship between the major and minor leagues.

Minor league teams are classified according to the skill level of their players. From highest to lowest, the leagues are classified as: AAA (American Association, International, Mexican, and Pacific Coast Leagues); AA (Eastern, Southern, and Texas Leagues); Advanced A (California, Carolina, and Florida State Leagues); A (Midwest and South Atlantic Leagues); Short Season A (New York-Penn and Northwest Leagues); Advanced Rookie (Appalachian and Pioneer Leagues); and Rookie (Arizona, Dominican Summer, and Gulf Coast Leagues). Except for the AAA level, the leagues are concentrated in geographic areas, with the location usually indicated by the league name. Schedules for the full-season leagues (AAA through A level) are about 140 games beginning in early April and ending, except for play-offs, at the end of August. Short season A level teams begin in mid-June and play about 76 games, while 68 and 60 games are scheduled for the rookie-advanced and rookie levels, respectively.

Five of the full-season leagues are located completely, or almost so, in the southern United States. These are the Florida State League (advanced A), the South Atlantic, or Sally League (A), the Carolina League (advanced A), the Southern League (AA), and the Texas League (AA). The individual clubs of these five leagues were the focus of my summer's route through Dixie.

In any given year, about 5,500 players perform in the minor leagues. In an average year, major league clubs sign 1,500 new players and assign almost all of them to a minor league club. In 1993, only four active players in the major leagues had not played minor league ball (Dave Winfield, Pete Incaviglia, Jim Abbott, and John Olerud). Of that large number of hopefuls, only 5 percent ever suit up in a major league clubhouse. While all minor leaguers have dreams, the reality is that most exist only to provide competition for the few major league prospects and entertainment for local fans.

The Professional Baseball Agreement (PBA) now in force was signed in 1990 and ratified in 1991. This document makes the major league clubs responsible for minor league player, manager, and coach assignments and pay, while minor league clubs (almost all are affiliated with a major league club) negotiate stadium facilities with counties or municipalities, provide local staff to run the clubs, and pay away-from-home travel expenses. The PBA is a far-ranging document, providing rules for such specifics as television revenue sharing and age limits of players at different levels. The current agreement expires September 30, 1997.

Behind Al Lang Stadium on the bay in St. Petersburg, the National Association resides in a one-story building, which is actually a remodeled clubhouse. As I walked toward the door, the blue water of the marina across the street bore bobbing sailboats whose frapping lines merged with the sounds of screeching seagulls. A soft breeze stirred leaves in the palm trees, and the sky was a brilliant blue. I stopped by to talk with Bob Sparks, the association's executive director for special projects, partly to thank him personally for the substantial support he had given me in providing access to the association's ballparks and press facilities during the 1993 season, and to find out if there were any new directions or issues in baseball I should know about.

In Bob's view, the major issues separating minor and major league baseball had already been negotiated, and little was likely to change the next time the agreement reached the table. I asked him about the new independent leagues beginning play in 1993 and 1994. These three new leagues, the Northern in the central north states and Canada, the Texas-Louisiana, and the Frontier in the Appalachian region were throwbacks to the minors of forty years ago when teams, and sometimes entire leagues, operated independent of major league working arrangements, trying to develop players and sell their contracts on the market to a major league team.

"Will the association make overtures to get them into the fold, or will they have to apply to you?"

"The latter," he said. "The problem is that it's tough to make it as an independent, and there are no more affiliations with major league clubs to be had. Some [major league] clubs are even talking about downsizing more, trying to get by with five instead of six or more farm clubs. Maybe going from two A level clubs to one."

The farm system had already changed dramatically. Before the reclassification of 1962, major league clubs might have had as many as seven hundred minor leaguers under contract and would invite them all to spring training. The St. Louis Cardinals, pioneers in the use of minor league clubs as a farm system, once had entire class D minor leagues under their control.

Despite the inevitable shifts of clubs and experimental new leagues, the minors had carved out a new niche in organized baseball in the past few decades, and little was likely to change in the near future.

11

I left Florida's west coast driving toward the midsection on small roads. In Winter Haven, I passed the empty ballpark that had for years been the spring training home of the Boston Red Sox. Each spring had brought Ted Williams down to show the youngsters how to swing a bat the Teddy Ballgame way. After a dispute with city officials about the stadium, the Red Sox moved to Fort Myers in 1992. The Cleveland Indians trained in Winter Haven in 1993, with their future spring training site still uncertain. Winter Haven's franchise in the Florida State League moved to Fort Lauderdale, and the Yankees, who were affiliated with the Lauderdale franchise for years, decided not to field a Florida State team in 1993. In an unrelated move, the Kansas City Royals entry moved from the carnival-like setting of Baseball City to Daytona. This confusing state of affairs led to what every league tries to avoid, an uneven number of teams for the year. With thirteen teams, six teams played each other on a given day, and the odd team was forced into an off day. It was hard to rotate pitchers, make travel arrangements, and get nonpitchers enough times at bat with so many off days.

I had arranged to have lunch in Orlando with a friend and because I was running a little late, tried to save time by driving the tiniest distance down the wrong side of a divided highway before making a turn. A Florida state highway patrolman, bothered by this creative move, laboriously wrote out a ticket, which made me even later for lunch.

I arrived at the designated meeting place apologetic, and piqued, mostly at myself.

"It's all right," said Ellen. "I'm always late myself when I try to go anywhere in a strange city."

She listened sympathetically to my biased version of the ticket encounter, and with patience and politeness managed to calm me down.

"I should have warned you about the highway patrol in Florida," she said. "They can be so . . . exacting." She was the first familiar face I had seen in over a week, and brought the sudden realization that I had set myself up for three months of interaction with strangers.

"Ellen," I said, "I'm homesick."

Trying to be helpful, she said, "Well, you'll only be on the road for eighty more days or so."

Ellen took me to a Cuban restaurant nearby and gradually her good nature, the friendly ambience of the neighborhood cafe, and the good Cuban food began to turn the day around for me. When we ordered iced tea, the waiter asked if we wanted it sweet or unsweet, as they do in the South nowadays. Years ago, they just poured it out of a pitcher, thick as syrup.

As we ate black beans and rice, Ellen told me about growing up in a small town in northern Florida, away from the tourist trade, which was Florida's main industry today. She spoke with a soft southern accent, perfect for reinforcing the images of a rural, mostly vanished Florida of the past. One of my reasons for making the trip was to see if the old virtues of charm, grace, and manners that had been traditional still existed, or whether that part of the South was gone. Eventually it occurred to me that there they were, sitting across the table from me, sipping sweetened ice tea.

After lunch, as I drove through Orlando to Kissimmee to see the Osceola Astros play baseball, Sweetspot's AM radio honed in on radio station WHAL, which billed itself as a Christian news station; the newscasters referred to it as "The Good News Station." The good news disc jockey was talking about a traffic jam, which was bad news, but more useful than good news might have been. WHAL broadcast an unusual mix of music, news, weather, and Christian messages. ("We have a travel special this week. A free trip to heaven. See your local church on Sunday for details.") Between thirty-year-old songs, the broadcaster told jokes, quoted passages of scripture, and interpreted their meanings for contemporary life. Central Florida didn't look much like the Old South, but it was beginning to sound like it.

Since it was still too early to go to the ballpark, I drove into downtown Kissimmee, home of the Osceola Astros. I was early, and decided to kill some time by asking about the local ball team. My hastily designed survey consisted of going into six business establishments and asking the same question: "How do I get to the park where the Osceola Astros play?" The question wasn't entirely gra-

13

tuitous; I had the general bearing from my *Baseball America Directory*, but didn't know the exact location.

The answers:

1. "They aren't here anymore. They left about a week ago." (This was a reference to the Houston Astros having completed spring training.)

2. "I think they're somewhere up in Orlando."

3. "I don't know." (This was a girl in an ice cream store, who then offered to call her boyfriend to find out. She thought he had been to a game once.)

4. "Which school? There are three."

5. "If they play where I think they play, take 192 east and it'll be on your left." (He was right, although he said he had never been to a game there.)

I concluded my highly unscientific survey by asking the question of a middle-aged couple who were leaving a store. They looked at each other blankly. "We're not from here," the woman said. "We're from Orlando." Orlando is about twenty miles north of Kissimmee.

I decided that I wouldn't have a lot of trouble finding a seat at the stadium that evening.

Osceola County Stadium was similar to others I had seen in the Florida State League. Fences were deep (330 feet to left and right, 410 feet to center, twin 390 feet power alleys) and everything on and off the field was symmetrical. Here, though, even the most ubiquitous symbols of minor league baseball were missing. The outfield fence was green mesh instead of the brightly painted signs that everywhere else lend a splash of color and character to the green and brown of the diamonds. Cypress trees beyond the right field fence helped soften the angular, regular lines a little.

I went up to the press box to pick up a media packet of player statistics. The general manager, Tim Bawmann, was on his walkie-talkie instructing an assistant to start checking tickets. A few hundred fans were in attendance, and almost all of them were in box seats, many, Tom guessed, illicitly. Whatever other reasons they might have had, fans weren't staying away because of ticket prices:

$3.50 for box seats, $2.50 for general admission, and $1.50 for seniors and children.

I spent the evening talking with Chris White, an Astros' pitcher who was charting pitches from a seat behind home plate. The next day's starting pitcher usually logs pitches to help familiarize him with the other team's hitters. Chris had worked the opener three days ago, going six innings with no decision, giving up three hits and one run.

"The [pitching] coach has us on a pitch count," he explained. "Eighty pitches and you're out of there, no matter what the situation."

Chris, a friendly, good-looking right-hander with a typical baseball build, six feet even, 180 pounds, had been drafted while in college in the twentieth round of the June 1991 draft by the Houston organization. Just short of age twenty-four, he was in his third year in professional baseball. In the New York–Penn short season league in 1991, he appeared mainly as a reliever. In 1992, as a starter for the Asheville Tourists in the South Atlantic league, Chris had gone 13–4 with a 3.38 earned run average. Both years he had excellent strike out-to-walk ratios, but the Astros were bringing him along slowly. Many of the current Osceola Astros had been at Asheville the year before and had been promoted together.

As we talked, Chris said all the right things about having a lot to learn about pitching but I was impressed with what he already knew. I talked him into playing a game by covering up the radar gun he was using to log the Astro pitcher's velocity and having us both guess speeds. Fastballs, consistently in the upper eighties, breaking ninety occasionally, were fairly easy, but curves and change-ups were harder. I would sometimes misjudge their speeds by up to ten miles per hour, but Chris hardly needed the gun.

"I was only over ninety once in the opener," he offered.

I asked if it bothered him to pitch to empty stands.

"I have to stay focused the same whether they're empty or full," he said. But then he told me about pitching before twenty thousand fans once in a summer league game. "I was pumped," he admitted.

Chris was born and lived awhile in Richmond, Virginia, which made him a southerner. He moved with his family, however, to

15

Greenville, Pennsylvania, in the northwest part of the state. He attended Cleveland State College and was articulate and well informed. At one point, he asked me, "Are you just a writer or do you have another profession?"

I told him that I was a college professor.

"I knew it," he said. "I can spot them." He should be able to; his father is a professor of philosophy at Teal College. Unlike most players I met during the trip, Chris seemed genuinely interested and asked a lot of questions about what I was doing. When I mentioned that I was going all the way to El Paso, he said "Why don't you just hang around Kissimmee all summer and write about the Osceola Astros drive to the Florida State pennant?"

I looked around at the smattering of deathly quiet fans and shuddered. "I'll just mosey on out west," I told him.

The Astros ran a couple of contests during the game. One was to guess the attendance. "Can't anyone just walk around for a few minutes and count the attendees?" I asked Chris. The crowd was announced a few innings later at 327, but by that time I would have challenged anyone to produce more than 100 bodies. Another contest featured the team mascot, Quazzie. Quazzie was supposed to represent something about the space program to reflect Houston's astronaut theme. The mascot wore a large orange fuzzy costume and was on the cover of the souvenir program ("QUAZZIE ENTERTAINS ALL FANS WITH HIS CRAZY ANTICS.") A ten-year-old boy raced Quazzie around the bases between innings. The prize, a free meal at Hooters, a restaurant chain featuring scantily clad waitresses and a full bar, seemed like an odd choice to offer a ten-year-old, but he won it. The kid really ran fast.

The players I met on the trip were a mixed bag, as were the nonplayers. I later exchanged a few words with another young man about the same age as Chris. I was sitting in the dugout during batting practice when he came off the field and threw his glove down on the bench next to where I was sitting. I picked it up and said "Gloves are bigger than they used to be when I played."

"When was that?" he asked absently.

"Oh, back in the twenties." That would have made me at least ninety years old.

16

"Hey. Long time ago," he said, his eyes vacantly following the line drives coming out of the batting cage.

I picked up State Highway 19 north of Orlando and drove through the Ocala National Forest. The rivers and creeks ran dark from the tannin leaching out of the pine tree roots. I stopped for a quick lunch of yogurt, fruit, and granola near a boat ramp on the Oklawaha River. Water lilies covered the surface of the dusky water and Spanish moss draped the trees that overhung the river banks. After eating I walked over to a quiet pool downstream from the ramp. An elderly man wearing bib overalls was fishing there. We talked for a minute and he showed me a spot in the water near a stump where he'd seen a "nigger man settin' here yesterday pullin' 'em in fast as he could throw his line back out."

The word rolled off his tongue as if it were neutral, like any other word in his description. The disturbing part wasn't that there was malice behind the epithet "nigger," but that there was no apparent feeling at all. I cut the conversation short and walked back to Sweetspot. Soon afterwards, I began chiding myself for running away. I had come to see if the Old South was still there, and when one of the darker parts of it had surfaced, had indignantly turned my back.

Ellen and the old fisherman represented, at least for me, two extremes of the southern tradition. And I knew that I wouldn't find an honest answer to the question of the South's character by walking away from any part of the Dixie heritage.

17

of Professional Baseball Leagues was in place and order became the rule. Fifty-two leagues began the 1910 season, a high-water mark until the late 1940s. World War I caused an attrition of leagues, but the 1920s produced a postwar boom, which hitched a ride on the prosperous economy and the good fortunes of major league baseball after the lively ball was introduced. The economic depression of the 1930s struck minor league baseball hard; by 1933, only fourteen leagues were in operation. But the advent of night baseball provided cheap entertainment, and the establishment of minors as farm systems and major league ownership of minor league players became permanent during the depression. World War II disrupted minor league baseball again as it did other aspects of life in the country. In 1942, such longstanding leagues as the Florida State and the Evangeline folded in the South, and by 1943, only nine leagues in the entire country completed the season. After World War II, minor league baseball reached its zenith. By 1949, fifty-nine leagues were in operation, with thirty-one, more than half the total, located in the South or Southwest. Georgia alone had entries in three class D leagues, the Georgia State, Georgia-Alabama, and Georgia-Florida Leagues.

After World War II, returning southern soldiers had a pocketful of money but the production of houses, new appliances, and new cars still lagged behind demand, leaving people with dollars to spend on recreation. Every small southern town had a movie theater and a pool hall to siphon off available entertainment dollars, but many towns as small as one or two thousand could also boast minor league teams. They were often at the lowest classification but provided a place to sit in the open air, an important consideration before air conditioning. Postwar attendance swelled, producing a golden age of the minor leagues. Over forty million fans went through the turnstiles in minor league parks annually in the late 1940s, and nationwide over four hundred towns fielded and supported teams. In small Georgia towns like Vidalia, Valdosta, Americus, and Waycross, folding wooden signs would be put out on a main intersection on summer mornings announcing "Game Tonight," with the time and name of the local baseball park. Sometimes the parks had no names; in the small southern town, there was no real need for a formal designation.

The bubble burst with disastrous results for the minors beginning in the early 1950s, in a way that almost no one had foreseen. When I first began attending minor league games in Tulsa around 1950, the infrastructure was already beginning to decay, though few realized it at the time. Gradually, televised major league games drew attention away from local teams, suburbanization drew people physically away from downtown ball parks, and the growing popularity of professional football combined to produce a sharp decline in minor league baseball that lasted for a quarter century. In 1962, the lowest levels of minor league baseball leagues (classifications B, C, and D) were abolished. This was the final admission that small towns couldn't, or wouldn't, support minor league ball. The goal for organized baseball eventually became to have one hundred minor league clubs survive, as feeders of the major league organizations—just one-fourth the number of teams that had flourished in the late forties.

Again, unpredicted, the late 1970s saw a resurgence in minor league baseball's popularity. Many, myself included, became disillusioned with major league baseball in the 1980s and discovered, or rediscovered, the game at a simpler, purer level. For others, it may have been just an extension of a gradual resurgence of interest at the major league level. Attendance picked up once more in minor league parks, but with several differences. By the early 1990s, twenty-six million fans were attending games, but the number of cities with teams was still small compared to the pretelevision years. No longer was simply announcing that a baseball game would be played enough to market the product. Minor league games were now part of an entertainment package, and front office club officials were more comfortable in discussing promotions and target populations than in detailing the caliber of team play.

Waycross, Georgia, had fielded minor league teams periodically from 1906 through 1963, when the Georgia-Florida League folded. In the nineteenth century, it had been known as the "crossing of the ways" because several railroad lines intersected there. I drove into town prepared to spend hours locating its last professional ballpark but was pleasantly surprised to see what could only have been a minor league baseball stadium standing prominently off the highway near the center of town. Memorial Stadium reposed like a grand brick and concrete relic, refreshingly quaint and archaic compared to the amorphous new parks of Florida.

The stadium was in use; its parking lot hosted a used car market. Sonny Bland, who worked for the city and was in charge of the stadium, was working there as I drove up. I asked if it would be okay to wander through and take some pictures, and he gave me a brief history of the park. It had been built in 1948 and '49 during the postwar heyday of minor league baseball. The concrete and steel construction indicated a feeling of permanence and surety that minor league baseball would always be a part of the city, an understandable feeling in those last few pretelevision years. The grandstand roof was in good repair and steel supporting posts had been made deliberately thin to minimize obstruction of sight lines. The most surprising feature was size. Sonny said that twelve thousand could be accommodated in stationary seats, and up to fifteen thousand when temporary chairs were added. Its major use today was for high school football but even in a football configuration, the old park was obviously meant as a place to see the summer game. Waycross's chamber of commerce had been trying to attract a minor league baseball club, but had run up against the usual problem. Without a player development contract from a major league team, professional baseball simply was not realistic in the 1990s.

As I headed up US 84 toward Savannah, the AM radio cracked and weather forecasters warned of tornadoes in southern Georgia. Fields had been plowed for planting and dust devils swirled across the highway. Here on the coastal plain the soil was dark, not the red clay common to the hill country of northern Georgia. Rain slapped the windshield, the wind bearing the clouds northeast in the same direction I was going. I wasn't sure that there would be a game in Savannah that evening. The clouds were ominous, dense with vertically developed shapes, like those that can drop a twister at any time.

An hour before game time, however, the weather had improved

somewhat. The approach to Arthur Grayson Stadium in Savannah was through wide streets lined with live oaks, shrouded in Spanish moss. Beautiful Greek Revival mansions, many of them antebellum, were set back from the street amidst parklike landscaping. The well-seasoned baseball field, built in 1925, was a small, red-brick structure lying partly hidden by moss draped from the many trees accommodated by unpaved squares in the concrete parking lot. Inside, seats were painted red and blue, and beyond the left and center-field walls a large stand of pines formed a backdrop. Because of its picturesque presentation, Grayson Stadium was one of the parks used in director John Badham's 1976 movie about the Negro Leagues, *The Bingo Long Traveling All-Stars and Motor Kings.*

The left-field fence was 290 feet from home plate, but the short distance had been legitimized somewhat by a wire screen about twenty feet high and extending along the fence for approximately 100 feet. The right-field line was 310 feet. Power alleys were not marked but were fairly deep. With a 400-foot drive necessary to carry the center field fence, home runs weren't particularly cheap unless pulled directly down the right-field line.

The Savannah Cardinals, a St. Louis farm club, were not one of minor league baseball's most affluent franchises. Attendance in 1992 was under eighty thousand, which put them near the bottom of the South Atlantic League. A temporary building lying just inside the gates to the stadium housed the club offices. This was the season's first Bleacher Bum Night, a promotion in which for $5.00, "bums" could go to the picnic area beside the left field foul line and enjoy an hour of unlimited hot dogs and beer. Afterward, they weaved over to the left field bleachers and sat down, looking groggy. I went to the concession stand instead and had a jalapeno hot dog (hot!) for two dollars, a beer (tepid) for two dollars, and a box of popcorn (cold) for one dollar.

The press box at Grayson was a flimsy affair reached by climbing stairs at the top of the grandstand and walking across a catwalk to a small compartment with two tiny booths hanging from the roof like a cabin on a dirigible. Three men ran everything. One kept score, the second served as public address announcer and scoreboard operator, and the third played the organ. No press was to be seen, though the *Savannah Morning News* carried an article on the game the following morning.

"Where's the play-by-play person?" I asked.

"No radio," one answered.

Until the game began, they occupied themselves with passing around a pair of binoculars, focusing on various women in the stands, and commenting, usually unfavorably, about their physical attributes.

When the game began, the Hickory Crawdads began crawling all over the Savannah Cardinals. The Crawdad pitcher, Mickey McKinnon, had his slider working well. He kept it at the batters' knees, coaxing groundouts and strikeouts. In the second, a Hickory batter lined a solo home run just inside the left field foul pole over the screen, and they later added an unearned run, blanking Savannah 2–0.

The three club employees began eating boiled peanuts, delivered from a concession stand. They threw the dusky shells on the floor, and in a few minutes the press box looked like it had an infestation of cockroaches. Wind whistled into the small booth, which vibrated and swayed noticeably every time a gust hit it broadside.

"Does it always feel like this up here?" I asked.

"Hell, this ain't nothin'," said the scorer.

In a few minutes, and obviously for my benefit, he said casually to the PA announcer, "Did you know this box ain't held on by nothin' but two bolts?"

The combination of the jalapeno dog (hot!) and the sickly swaying of the press box was producing more than a mild nausea. I got up, stomach churning, and tried to navigate the catwalk without looking down.

Solid ground and fresh air brought some equilibrium to my system, so I walked out to the left field bleachers. In the seventh inning, thirty-five or forty "bums" remained, and, surprisingly, considering their red, bleary eyes, were talking baseball. A woman noticing my camera with a long lens and lens hood, started shouting for me to take her picture. I did, and this prompted several other requests. To save film, I just pretended to shoot pictures and faked cocking the rewinder. Everyone was happy and I asked several people about the teams' prospects, receiving foggy predictions filtered through the haze of a heavy beer promotion.

Outside Savannah the next morning, I stopped for breakfast in a truck stop and sat at the counter next to a large, rough-looking trucker. I ordered a cheese omelet, grits, and biscuits, and the trucker ordered toast and coffee. When the waitress returned with the orders she looked at us, looked at the plates, gave him the omelet and me the toast. We sorted out our orders and began talking. More accurately, he told me almost his entire life story in about twenty minutes, while smoking four cigarettes, and I ate breakfast and listened. He was, like myself, a fringe southerner by birth, but had lived and worked in the South much of his life and spoke with a pronounced southern accent. He had the fierce autonomy of not only the southern white male but also the independent trucker, the "last cowboy." The incidents he related from his life all ended the same way. Someone offended him and he summarily told them to "Kiss my ass!" One unsettling story concerned a company he worked for several years ago, which developed a voluntary retirement plan, and he decided that it cost too much. In his words, "I told them they could kiss my ass on that retirement plan. What good is a retirement plan that costs so much that I cain't feed my wife and kids when I'm not retired?"

The *Savannah Morning News* box score announced the attendance of the previous evening's game as 718. This must have included season ticket holders who hadn't attended the game, but it had been a large crowd compared to the Florida State League games I had attended. Furthermore, the Savannah fans, only seven games into the season, had learned the names of the players and were vocal and rowdy, a change from the hushed ballpark atmospheres in Florida.

Savannah is a member of the class A South Atlantic, or Sally League, whose teams I would be visiting over the next few weeks. The league was formed in 1904 and ran, with the usual interruptions for wars and the depression, at the class C, then B, and finally A levels up through 1962. Small cities in Georgia and the Carolinas comprised its main membership, with a few entries over the years from Alabama, Tennessee, Virginia, and West Virginia. In the early 1960s, the old Southern Association folded and the new Southern League was formed from the South Atlantic League's cities. Later a new Sally League at the A level became successor of the Western Carolinas League in 1980 and had been active since. In 1993, the league had fourteen entries divided into northern and southern divisions and stretched from Hagerstown, Maryland, to Albany in southwest Georgia. Some of the oldest, smallest and most unusual baseball parks in professional baseball are in the Sally League, many of which I would see in the next few weeks.

Out of Savannah, I dropped down to state highway 144 and drove across the middle of Georgia toward Macon. In Glenville, I saw my first Confederate flag on the trip, flying in front of the high school. In the small towns, houses had front porches with swings, and sidewalks framed well-kept lawns. The front porch was an almost perfect solution to socializing in the small southern town, a transition between inside and outside. Sitting on the swing in the evening welcomed those who were out walking to stop and chat for awhile, and relieved the hosts from inviting the strollers inside. Many of the houses had huge banks of azaleas in the front yards, and in mid-April they were in full bloom.

Vidalia, famous for onions, had a minor league team in the class D Georgia State League from 1948 through 1956, so I stopped to inquire about the fate of the baseball park. After several false leads, I learned the names of two former players who still lived in town and telephoned them. Nothing remains of the ballpark today, I was assured. Its location was now part of a strip of fast-food restaurants and new car showrooms; the park, which either didn't have a name or the name has been forgotten, was torn down to provide parking for K-Mart and Piggly Wiggly stores. I heard some good stories about the old teams though, including the fact that Mays Dobbins' career ended because of overindulging in ham and redeye gravy before playing on a hot summer afternoon. Richard Herring remembered that the park was shared by a "nigra" team, whose players, he thought, were more talented than those on the white professional team. I didn't like finding out, though, that one of the diamonds of Dixie was buried under a K-Mart parking lot.

Macon, Georgia, was one of the jewels of the South. The city was laid out southwest of the Ocmulgee River, and the older residential sections overlooked the downtown business district from a sizeable hill. Many of the large homes on the hill were antebellum mansions spared by Sherman on his destructive trek to the sea. I put aside my guidebook because there was so much of interest not mentioned, and hiked back and forth across the hill taking in the Old South scenery. The buildings were a broad mix of nineteenth- and twentieth-century styles, from stately Greek Revivals to a snappy art deco launderette at the edge of the commercial district. The azaleas and dogwoods were in bloom, framing the houses with those most southern of blossoms. On Mulberry Street, I passed the Old Cannonball House, which took a Union round during the war, and on High Street the birthplace of Sidney Lanier, Georgia's greatest poet. Macon was a bonus, and reminded me that not all the diamonds of Dixie have four bases and smell like hot dogs.

Luther Williams Field in Macon was the main park used for filming *The Bingo Long Traveling All-Stars and Motor Kings*. The film concerned the period just before integration of professional baseball, and the two main characters, played by James Earl Jones and Billy Dee Williams, were based loosely on Josh Gibson and Satchel Paige. Outfield fence signs were covered in green for the film, and a few other atmospheric changes were made, but the park needed little modification to serve as a period piece. Seating capacity was only 3,700 and besides the grandstand, which ended between home and the corner bases, only a small set of tin bleachers extended down the right field line. Although there were eight light stanchions, each had only eight lights, adding to the quaint, old-fashioned look of the park.

I went out to the field several hours before game time to watch batting practice. The Columbus (Ga.) Redstixx were in town, and looking through their media notes, I spotted the name of a player whose hometown was listed as Potomac, Maryland. Derek Hacopian and I lived only a few miles apart in Maryland, and I looked him up when batting practice was finished. He seemed glad to talk with someone from home. Derek was dark, handsome, and frequently flashed a pleasant smile. This was his second year in pro-

27

fessional baseball. He had been drafted in 1992 after establishing solid athletic credentials at Churchill High School in Potomac, then at Montgomery College and the University of Maryland, where he was Atlantic Coast Conference player of the year and an all-American. In the short season New York-Penn League in 1992, he had hit a respectable .311 with nine home runs and forty-six runs batted in. He seemed disappointed in how the current year was going, appearing in five of the eight games with only sixteen at bats, and hitting .250. "And I'm DHing a lot." I promised to stay in touch and follow his progress throughout the season.

Before I even left the Sally League a few weeks later, his name had started appearing in the top ten in batting statistics. At season's end, Derek had a .315 batting average, good for third in the league, with twenty-four home runs and eighty-two runs batted in. He continued to be used in the designated hitter role, however, and by midseason the media were regularly referring to Derek Hacopian as "D.H. the DH."

In Macon, I concentrated on talking to ballplayers' relatives and significant others. Beverly Hatcher attended a game to watch her fiance, Terrence Brock, perform as Macon's starting pitcher. She was a Florida State University student, close to graduation, pretty and blond, and not really a baseball fan at all. She and Terrence had been engaged for six years, since high school. First college and now his career had delayed marriage. She wanted to go to law school, but was uncertain about her fiance's baseball future and whether to postpone her own career. The immediate plan was for her to spend the summer working in Macon where Terrence pitched, and then to evaluate how things were going.

At Florida State, Terrence Brock had been a right fielder. He switched positions after Atlanta drafted him in 1992, in the twelfth round, and went 6–4 with a 2.31 earned run average for Idaho Falls, a rookie league team. Despite Terrence's good beginning, Beverly seemed realistic about the long odds of making it to the major leagues. We were sitting together and talking five or six rows up behind home plate. "I hope he doesn't think I'm hitting on you and let it affect his pitching," I said.

She laughed. "He's so focused on the mound, I don't think he even knows I exist while he's pitching."

She may have been right. He went five innings, allowed two hits, no runs, struck out six, and didn't come looking for me after the game.

Next game one of the staff told me that Terrell Buckley's family was in the stands. I asked his small crowd of relatives if I could sit through the game with them and ask a few questions about Terrell. His mother, sister, cousin, and fiance were in town for the weekend from Pascagoula, Mississippi, a ten-hour drive to Macon. They all planned to see Terrell play as often as possible during the season.

Terrell grew up in Pascagoula and emerged as a two-sport athlete, although his baseball experience was limited. Last season (1992), he had been an all-rookie cornerback for the National Football League's Green Bay Packers. The Atlanta Braves, who seem to be partial to football players despite the Deion Sanders experience, drafted Terrell out of Florida State University in the thirty-eighth round. Their interest was based on his basic athletic ability rather than proven baseball skills, for Terrell had only thirteen at bats and two hits in his college career. After the June draft, there was no time to play him in a rookie or short season A league because of training camp with the Packers, so he missed the 1992 baseball season. He trained with the Braves in West Palm Beach in spring 1993, and they were impressed enough with his ability to assign him to a class A team, agreeing to his reporting for summer camp with the Packers in July. Terrell had signed for a reported $6.2 million with Green Bay. His monthly pay with the Macon Braves was $850.

No one in Terrell's family had any doubt that he would be in the majors within three years. They had seen his success with the Packers and had spent years reading positive publicity about his superb athletic skills, and assumed that baseball stardom would come easily. That evening, however, Terrell was hitting .190 and had struck out six times in twenty-one times at bat. I asked Laura Buckley, his mother, whether she would rather Terrell had finished college before signing with the Packers.

"Whatever he wants, that's what I want for him," she said.

29

His fiance, Denise Ramirez, was a little more forthcoming.

"Frankly, big-time sports is where the big bucks are. They aren't in having a college degree by your name."

As a Ph.D. driving around the country in a twenty-one-year-old pickup, I was in no position to argue with her.

About a week later, I caught up with Terrell in Columbia, South Carolina, and met him after the game in his hotel room. He had a sliding "strawberry," a circular scrape on his hip about two inches in diameter, and had undressed because of the discomfort from clothing.

"Sometimes," he said a little self-consciously, "these things hurt more than real injuries."

Terrell Buckley was a handsome, even featured black man with two wide gold chains around his neck. At 5'10" and a muscular 175 pounds, he seemed to have the ideal build for baseball—compact, powerful, and speedy. In the batting cage, though, he hadn't appeared comfortable that afternoon, fouling off batting practice speed pitches despite his obviously good bat speed and command of the entire plate. He couldn't get in a groove with consistent solid contact, and his timing just wasn't there. I asked if the switch to a wooden bat from the aluminum bats, which were standard in college and high school, had a big effect.

"No, but I didn't play enough in college to get that used to an aluminum bat." He admitted, though, that this year was the first time at any baseball level where the greater precision required by wood was a factor. He had only one extra-base hit and was striking out a lot.

I hadn't seen Terrell play enough to judge his skills in the outfield, but on routine flies during batting practice, he seemed to be nonchalant, even appearing to loaf. When a ball was hit over his head, however, a glimpse of the instincts necessary to make a good outfielder flashed unmistakably.

"I'm a cornerback," he said. "I don't have any trouble breaking back on a ball." The only part of his game of concern, he claimed, was lack of arm strength on throws from the outfield to home plate. "But that will come."

The longer we talked, the more obvious it became that his central identity and interest was in football. Terrell said, though, that he was giving himself three years to make the major leagues, and if he did, he wanted to play both sports as long as possible. He was adjusting to the travel required by professional baseball, but didn't like it. Also, he seemed annoyed at the length of the baseball season.

"Why," he asked me seriously, "is a baseball season so long?"

That was a hard question for me to answer, because I had always considered a baseball season too short.

Things were in disarray at Paul Eames Sports Complex in Albany, Georgia, when I arrived. The previous evening had seen the first South Atlantic League game at the brand new stadium, and the front office staff had just moved into its new offices. I saw unpacked boxes and smelled fresh paint everywhere, the police were meeting in the unpaved parking lot about traffic patterns, and the sod on the field had only been down for two weeks. It hadn't taken yet and the grass was a dull shade somewhere between green and tan. Only on the field did anything seem normal, as the players and coaches followed familiar, reassuring rituals: stretch, jog, hit, field, run the bases.

The Albany Polecats were scheduled that evening to play the Charleston Rainbows in their second home game of the season. This was Albany's second season in the league, and there was high excitement and enthusiasm in the city over the return of professional baseball after an absence of thirty-four years. "Polecats" is an unlikely nickname because of the reputation of skunks, but Albany teams of the past had a tradition of colorful names. From 1911 to 1916, a team in the earlier class B Sally League was nicknamed "Babies" because Albany was the smallest city in the circuit; and from 1926 to 1928, the team was known as the Albany "Nuts" because of the local pecan industry.

Lorie Baran, the director of press box operations officially, and about one hundred other things unofficially, was assigned to sponsor me and probably keep me out of other people's hair. Despite the overall dither, the staff was friendly and was having fun, taking the move in stride and generally laughing about the numerous shakedown problems.

On a separate page, Isham and another witness, R. F. Hannah, jointly swear to the following answers:

2. Are you acquainted with Henry W. Renfro, the applicant, if so how long have you known him?

Answer: We have known him 32 or 33 years.

4. Do you know of his having served in the Confederate army or the Georgia militia? How do you know this?

Answer: Applicant served in the Confederate army we served in the same company and regiment.

5. When, where and in what company and regiment did he enlist?

Answer: In Oct 1861 at Sweetwater Tenn in Co A of 62 Tennessee.

6. Were you a member of the same company and regiment?

Answer: We was.

7. How long did he perform regular military duty, and what do you know of his service as a Confederate soldier, and the time and circumstances of his discharge from the service?

Answer: For over 2 years he was a good Soldier we dont remember as to his discharge the time and place.

On his application, Henry had sworn that he was in the Confederate army "until the surrender." Other forms attached to the application indicate that it was successful. The deposition for witnesses had been signed by Isham in his own hand, so he had been literate, unlike my grandfather.

In all I had learned little about my great-grandfather's life. No records had been uncovered to document the campaigns he had fought, the quality of his service, or even the military rank he had achieved. Census records indicate that he married Rebecca and began having children after 1865, so he was apparently a Confederate soldier until the surrender also. That, and the fact that he had helped an old army buddy obtain a pension, was all that remained. He had been a hero to my grandfather, that much I remembered, and there was nothing in the records to indicate that this measure of the man was misplaced.

Out of Atlanta I headed east to get back to the heart of the region where South Atlantic League baseball is played. With no clear destination for the night, I drove awhile and stopped to make a telephone call. One of my colleagues in Maryland, Dennis Sullivan, had told me before the trip that Johnny Mize, the big first baseman who hit the long ball for three major league teams from 1936 to 1953, lived in retirement in Demorest, Georgia. I pulled off at a rest stop and called him. I got his answering machine, which said: "This is the John Mize residence. The Big Cat cain't come to the phone right now. Leave your name and telephone number, and if you're calling long distance, I will call you back collect." The Big Cat didn't intend to get stuck with a big telephone bill. Unfortunately, I didn't have a number to leave and decided to drive on and try later.

They called him "Big Cat" because of his agility around first base despite his considerable bulk. His quickness and fielding finesse stemmed from early experiences with tennis. He was good enough to win county championships and may have had a professional career in that sport had the baseball coach left him alone. John Robert Mize began playing college baseball in the northeast Georgia town of Demorest when he was only fourteen. I remembered his early-fifties career with the Yankees, when he was used mainly as a pinch hitter, and when he always seemed to deliver in the clutch. His Hall of Fame statistics were mostly accrued earlier with the Cardinals and Giants and included 2,011 hits and 359 career home runs. Despite a career lifetime .312 batting average, and career highs of fifty-one home runs in 1947 and a .364 batting average in 1937, he wasn't elected to the Hall of Fame until his twenty-third year of eligibility. At the induction, he said: "I had a speech ready but somewhere along in 28 years, it got lost."

I wanted to ask him about the early days when he played baseball in the South, before the big leagues. Although I finally reached him and he listened politely to my story, when I suggested coming by Demorest to talk with him, he firmly declined. "I just don't fool with it anymore," he said. John Mize was eighty years old, had been a public figure for sixty years, and had certainly earned the right to pass on an interview.

A month and a half later I read in *USA Today* that Johnny Mize had died the previous day of cardiac arrest at his home. I regretted

"Into Royston, to buy some ice."

"How long you going be in Georgia?"

I paused. These questions had nothing to do with checking for sobriety, and the tone was belligerent.

"I'll probably leave tomorrow."

"Sure you haven't had nothing to drink?"

I didn't answer. To hell with this, I thought. Let him arrest me for not answering the same question three times. He gave my identification one more canvassing and handed the two cards back.

"Sir," he said, "you'll git to Royston faster if you go to your right." His pronunciation of the last two words sounded like "Yore-rot," which I thought at first must be another town in Georgia.

"Where is that?"

He leaned back. "You don't know where your right is at?" He looked across the road at the other officer, as if in disbelief, and then pointed. "Take that road there."

I took the road on my right, but I didn't thank him for the information.

Royston was a small town surrounded by farms. Tractors bounced along the roads and pickups were the most numerous vehicle types in town. The main street was lined with one- and two-story brick buildings, the brick chipping and crumbling under the force of Georgia summers, approaching the same color as the red clay hills just beyond the city limits. References to Ty Cobb abounded in the town. A memorial granite bust stood in a sort of breezeway between two plain buildings used by the city. Diagonally across the street was Cobb Memorial Hospital, donated by the ballplayer late in his life in memory of his parents. I drove down Cobb Street, past small homes with wooden front porches and backyards plowed and readied for planting vegetable gardens. A dead opossum lay directly in the middle of the street. Cobb's name had obviously not brought hordes of tourists to Royston; I saw only one rundown motel on the outskirts of town.

No one interested in architectural style can possibly be bored in a new town. Even the smallest places boast one or two commercial buildings or residences of character and visual dignity. I had begun to think that Royston was an exception when I turned a corner and

44

saw a delightful American foursquare. The hipped-roof, two-story house had four rooms on each floor and a front porch running the full width of the house. Two large dormers punched out of the roof. This boxlike house type was common from the 1890s to the 1920s, but this was an unusually fine, unaltered specimen.

I reached for my camera lying on the seat in the pickup cab, and as I did, my peripheral vision picked up a city police cruiser moving slowly toward me. Two officers were staring intently, undoubtedly speculating about my motives in looking over the house. I left the camera on the seat and eased on down the street, hoping they wouldn't turn, flip on the blinkers, and pull me over. The conversation, I knew, would be predictable.

("Officer, I wasn't casing the joint. I was just admiring that colossal American foursquare."

"Well, sir, how about if we haul your colossal ass down to headquarters and talk about it.")

They kept driving slowly down the street, looking my way in the rearview mirror. I had been in Royston less than an hour and had been scrutinized by the police twice already.

Railroad tracks ran behind the row of stores on the eastern side of Main Street, and a carnival had been set up in a grassy field just beyond the tracks. After having dinner at my campsite in the state park, I drove back into Royston to see the carnival. At dusk the bright lights beckoned Royston's young, and the smells of corn dogs and cotton candy floated over the midway. Calliope music flowed from the mechanical rides and barkers hawked their haunted houses and exhibits of oddities.

City police were stationed at each end of the midway. I walked past one, carrying my camera, and he eyed me suspiciously. For a moment he looked as if he was going to stop me, but he said nothing. I was beginning to accept this as an unavoidable aspect of being in Royston. They were there, I suppose, for crowd control. The "crowd" looked to be about twenty people.

Grubby, haunted-looking teenagers worked the booths with games, extolling the virtues of their chalk animals and stuffed toys. I took a few pictures of the general scene, and was accosted by laughing teenagers offering to pose.

45

The carnival manager came over, probably assuming at first that I was a local reporter. He was a thin, grey-haired man of seventy-one, easy to talk to, with a keen sense of humor. He was surprised, he told me, to see so many people turn out because he hadn't been able to arrange advance publicity. After we talked awhile about the carnival business, I asked him about the working conditions of the young people. He said that they were much improved over the past. He tried to keep the same people for the season, but there was a lot of turnover. "I want it to be like a family," he said, "but they still come and go." He claimed that the trailers that hauled the equipment were converted to comfortable sleeping quarters during their stayovers in small towns. "They got a nice living space now," he said. "The truck trailers are fixed up, they got bunks, got a nice set up. Used to be they'd sleep wherever they could, under the trucks sometimes, wherever. Not like that any more. Like it was in the old days."

"When were the old days?" I asked.

"Not too long ago," he said.

I had felt uneasy since arriving in Royston. Not only had the police gone that extra mile to make me feel uncomfortable, but also other townspeople looked at me as an intruder. Yet I seemed to have all the right credentials—I was white, male, and drove a pickup truck. I could imagine the fear that would have been produced by driving into Royston forty or fifty years ago without those credentials.

Victoria Bryant State Park sits on a hilltop two miles west of Royston. The night was cool but clear and the stars were beautiful. Visibility out over the surrounding countryside was good, and I could see just how physically isolated Royston was. The xenophobic little town had shown me something interesting, though, after all. Tyrus Raymond Cobb's psyche, formed by the mosaic of life in this slice of rural Georgia, was now more understandable. The "Georgia Peach," probably the most ironic nickname ever affixed to a ballplayer, was no more admirable to me as a person but Royston had been like a looking glass reflecting his personality in all details.

Next morning, I looked at the road map after breakfast. I wanted to take state highway 17 to Elberton, then pick up 72 to South

Carolina. There was no realistic way to avoid driving through Royston again. I buckled my seatbelt, pulled on a billed cap that said "Scout" over the visor, and when the signs said SPEED LIMIT 30, dropped back to twenty-five. I drove slowly and soberly out of Georgia.

tempted "the wave," spurred on by the PA announcer. In the middle of the seventh, Rockin' Robert returned. This time he danced on the third base dugout, again to great applause. At the end of the seventh, a man in a Bombers uniform climbed on top of the first base dugout and led fans in singing "Take Me Out to the Ball Game."

After the top of the eighth, two contestants were chosen from the stands and were given bats. They were then required to put the ends of their bats on the ground, lower their foreheads to the knobs, and spin around ten times before running from home to first. They got dizzy, ran into each other, recovered somewhat, and began to pump their legs toward first but veered off sharply toward the dugout. This "dizzy bats" contest was one of the most popular at minor league parks. Although I wasn't sure why, I laughed hysterically along with everyone else each of the thirty or forty times I saw it happen.

Before the bottom of the eighth, the PA announcer told us that several three- and four-year-olds would dance on top of the third base dugout. They were called "Students of Rockin' Robert," who had himself been all of eight years old. As the "students" started tapping away to fast music, one tapped over dangerously close to the dugout edge. An adult lunged frantically to grab the little girl, then draped himself along the dugout edge from the other side to keep the children from falling off and ending the event in disaster. The kids tapped on obliviously, receiving enthusiastic applause.

Contests do sometimes end unfortunately. Later, during a dizzy bats race at a Double A park, I noticed club officials guarding the dugout entrance. I was told that on opening day a man had lost his balance after spinning around the bat and fell onto the concrete lip of the dugout, causing a concussion and requiring many stitches. Although the club might have been blamed, he didn't sue the organization. Fans at minor league games are participants in the evening entertainment in ways that are foreign to those who go to only major league games. Suing the ballclub would be like suing a good neighbor.

After the game, I caught the trolley to the upper end of the parking lot. The old car heaved and rocked, and parents kept protective

arms around their sleepy children. Older children examined souvenirs and young lovers held hands. Another minor league evening
was winding down.

I read an account of the game in the local newspaper the next
morning. There was nothing minor league about players' abilities
to handle baseball language. When asked to assess the game, Don-
nie White, one of the batting heroes in the 12–2 laugher, said:

"We started off slow [this season], and we're still struggling a
little hitting the ball, but we're putting it in play and beginning to
play much better."

How about their pitcher?

"Their pitcher was struggling."

Ron Washington, the Bombers' manager, was asked if it's easy
to let up when leading 12–2. Ron said:

"It doesn't matter what the score is. You go out there with one
attitude, and that's to play the game for nine innings."

4

Tobacco Fields of Dreams

WORLD WAR MEMORIAL STADIUM in Greensboro, North Carolina, was billed by its South Atlantic League baseball team, the Hornets, as the oldest minor league ballpark still in use in the country. This claim was, however, disputed. The major point of contention was that although the stadium opened in 1926, the first professional baseball game wasn't played there until 1930. Both Luther Williams Field in Macon, Georgia and Silver Stadium in Rochester, New York, opened for baseball in 1929 and were still in operation.

The field was built for football and track, and early distances down right- and left-field lines were very short. Originally, the foul pole in right field was only 248 feet from home plate. A half-mile dirt track ran down the left-field line and the original seating was in the form of a reversed J, with the stem paralleling the track.

The essential features of the park remain untouched. Fans enter under three Romanesque arches flanked by solid towers with pyramidal tops. The single-decked grandstand is concrete and seating capacity is 7,500. Distances are now a more conventional 327 feet down the lines and 401 feet to center. In 1993, two hundred gallons of paint and a cleaning of the interior cement had made the old park gleam without changing its intimacy and ambiance.

One aspect of the park is, at least to my knowledge, unique. A creek runs through it. Actually, the creek runs underneath it, entering under right field from about half way between first base and the foul pole to emerge outside the right center-field fence. The right fielder's normal position is almost exactly over the creek running a few feet below. I walked around the outside wall with John Frey, the Hornets' general manager, to see the phenomenon. The stream had deep cut banks so the builders had just laid the field over it from one bank to another. Outside the fence, where the watercourse emerged, John pointed. "Home runs often end up in here." Right on cue, a soggy baseball bobbed by in the current.

A few hours before game time, I met John Horshok, one of the Hornets' new owners. He walked up as Frey and I were sitting in the stands watching the ground crew work on the field. Rain had fallen earlier and washed out batting practice. John was a dynamic, energetic man who delivered one-liners in a sharp, staccato rhythm. He had been on the business end of the sports world for years in merchandising, promotion, and more recently, ownership. Before coming to Greensboro, he was in the restaurant business in northern Virginia with former Washington Redskin quarterback Joe Theismann. He told me that the buying price of the Greensboro Hornets had been $2.5 million, and that they had settled on April Fool's Day, just three weeks before.

"Do you think you bought in at the right time?" I asked him.

"Hell no. The right time was when the team cost $25,000, not two and a half million dollars."

The PBA required that every team have a single individual who was responsible for club decisions. This owner attended minor and major league meetings and was the community's visible symbol of ownership. The actual ownership structure was usually more complicated, however. The Greensboro team was owned by American Baseball Capital, Incorporated. The seven corporate members owned various amounts of the team. They were all checked out by the national association before settlement to assure that none of their other businesses—say, a local concession enterprise or one that had any connection to gambling—would represent a conflict of interest. Sufficient money was not the only criterion the association used to evaluate potential owners. Even the limited owners were invited to participate by the major money people because they had some connection with baseball. Tim Cullen, the executive vice president of the Hornets, was a former major league player with the Washington Senators. In the case of better-known celebrities, who have bought into several minor league teams (in Memphis, for example, movie actor/director Ron Howard is an owner), being a lifelong fan seemed to be connection enough. The association recognizes the media value of having a movie star or sports personality own a team.

As John Horshok said, the ideal time to buy a minor league team was in the past. The world of baseball is rife with stories about visionary entrepreneurs who bought franchises in the late seventies or early eighties for a few thousand dollars—or sometimes for simply taking over a team's debts—and sold them five years later for a few million. Even class A teams today sell for several million, and the consensus is that the big growth and appreciation in minor league clubs value has already occurred. However true this may be, John Horshok did not look unhappy to be an owner. He looked downright delighted.

His investment included a park alteration project, which had already started, and would be unique among baseball parks. The project, located beyond the left field bleachers, was the addition of a combination food court and museum.

By game time, rain had been falling off and on for an hour and a half. Baseball rules say that the authority to cancel a game rests with the home team until the lineup cards are exchanged, and then shifts to the umpires. After receiving the evening's cards, the umpires dutifully took a cursory walk through the sodden outfield (where water was standing several inches deep) and called the game. No one seemed in any hurry to leave, especially me, so I sat in the press box drinking beer and talking baseball as long as anyone would hang around. When you live in the back of a pickup truck, rainouts spawn feelings of boredom and claustrophobia. Owners like John Horshok see them more ominously, even as minor disasters, biting chunks from an already too skinny profit margin.

The rain had been pushed in on the leading edge of a cold front, and by morning the temperature had dropped noticeably. I found a laundromat in Greensboro and unloaded my bulging laundry bag. A restaurant across from the laundromat caught my eye because it resembled the homey cafe where I meet my fishing partner Doyle for breakfast before hitting the trout streams. The Greens-

and the owner asked me if I could pitch better if he slipped me more money. 'I don't know,' I told him, 'but I would sure feel better.' One fifty or two hundred [per month] was top salary for first-year men. I remember those payments now when I look at my social security records. There was no tax on the money, of course."

Five years after burning out his arm, Amby could still get a pitching job in professional baseball. What might have been, with today's knowledge and training methods, was interesting to speculate. His son, Barry, played on the little league and high school fields of Smithfield and was drafted third overall in the United States (the second high school player chosen) in the 1970 baseball draft. In one of those coincidences that sometimes occur in small towns, Amby's former manager in class D baseball was Barry's high school coach. Barry played ten years in the majors and after retiring in 1981, managed in the minors for several years. He eventually returned to the majors as a coach, and in 1993 was first base coach with the Mets.

While the old minor leaguers like Amby still rankle at their exploitation and say that professionally, if you don't make the big leagues, your career is meaningless, regret isn't something they convey in their stories or in the tone of their voices. They were paid for playing baseball, and my guess is that few would give up those years even if they somehow could.

Following Amby's directions, I drove to the old field, off Pitchi Road, and saw that it was now used for American Legion baseball. When Amby had played, the outfield fences had been wooden, had proper power alleys, and had measured 340'-390'-340'. Stands were larger then; for one play-off game in 1948, four thousand fans had attended. The park had no name, or at least none that Amby could remember. In 1954, a hurricane leveled the field and no baseball was played there for years until it was fixed up for amateur use. Crowds today are closer to forty than four thousand, and the crack of baseball on wooden bats has been replaced by the clang of aluminum, but the little field, still unnamed, clings to its original purpose.

5

The New Bull in Durham

THE CAROLINA LEAGUE HAS A shorter history than others in the South, but has been a stable and successful baseball confederation. It began as a class C league in 1945 and has operated in twenty-six cities. Two of the charter members, Winston-Salem and Durham, North Carolina, still field teams. In 1949, the league moved up a notch to class B, and in the 1962 reorganization gained a class A designation. Over time, it has evolved into a high or fast A league, as compared to the low A South Atlantic League. The current eight teams have a northern division comprised of Frederick (Maryland), Lynchburg (Virginia), Prince William (Virginia), Wilmington (Delaware), and a southern half of Durham, Kinston, and Winston-Salem (all in North Carolina), and Salem (Virginia).

The league's image was celebrated in the 1988 movie *Bull Durham*, filmed in Durham and other southern minor league cities. Some even credited the film with the resurgence of interest in minor league baseball, but attendance figures showed a healthy number of fans coming to minor league parks throughout the 1980s. Even if the film was primarily a reflection of the already rising interest in minor league ball, it helped make the Durham franchise one of the most famous in minor league history.

Grainger Stadium in Kinston was built in 1951 and still evokes the feeling of the 1950s. Blue is the theme color, covering the short fence around the front of the park and the steel girders that support a blue grandstand roof. The box seats are folding chairs. Distances run 335 feet to left and right and 390 feet to center. The whole

When minor league parks copy their big league progenitors, they nullify some of their built-in advantages. The best minor league parks I saw were pure and simple, erratic but democratic. Looking around the old Bulls' field I decided that, although the future Durham park would be photographed, written about, and marveled at, the new concrete bull just wouldn't snort quite the same as that rickety old plywood creation.

Next morning, a Sunday, I was driving along Stafford Road in Winston-Salem, North Carolina, looking for a place for breakfast when I saw three neon words glowing red. HOT DOUGHNUTS NOW. Actually, the word "now" was slanted across a doughnut between the words "hot" and "doughnut," so the sign read HOT NOW DOUGHNUTS. I jerked Sweetspot around in an illegal U turn and headed for the Krispy Kreme parking lot. I expected the drivers behind me to shout curses and flip me the bird, but they must have been familiar with this maneuver when the sign was red.

This was the first Krispy Kreme shop I had passed on the trip and I had the good luck to hit it when fresh, hot doughnuts were coming out of the oven. For those who only know Krispy Kreme doughnuts as the stiff, dated products sold by the Girl Scouts, reverence for the hot product may seem undue. The parking lot was crowded with cars of the educated, however, and had everything from a pickup even older than Sweetspot to a sleek black Lincoln Continental. I ordered a cup of coffee and a six pack of glazed and ate four of them in the shop. The waitress topped off customers' coffees and traded stories with the regulars. The glaze dripped and the sugar and fat melted like butter with every bite.

I told an assistant manager there was a Krispy Kreme shop in Alexandria, Virginia, not far from where I lived. He told me with some pride that the company was founded in Winston-Salem in 1937. The founder, Vernon Rudolph, bought a secret recipe from a Creole in the French Quarter of New Orleans and turned the yeast-raised results into a legend with a cult following spreading across the South. Now the one hundred plus shops dotted the Southeast in more than seventy cities, moving as far west as Memphis. The newer places had succumbed to modern trends—drive-through windows and standardized baking times. Traditionally, the doughnuts came out at unpredictable intervals and the red sign would flash randomly. Something will inevitably be lost, of course. The little shop sparkled with friendliness that Sunday morning, with chatter obviously as important as the sugar and carbohydrate-loaded objects that ostensibly brought everyone together.

Before leaving with my two uneaten doughnuts, I said to the assistant manager, "You must get a lot of questions about the history of Krispy Kreme."

"Not really," he said. "Most people just eat the doughnuts."

Swinging at the first pitch he was offered, Motorboat Jones of the Winston-Salem Spirits hit it on a line over the left center field wall at Ernie Shore Stadium. I was in attendance at a Sunday afternoon Carolina League game between the Spirits and the Wilmington Blue Rocks. Ernie Shore had proved to be one of the hardest to find baseball parks in the South. It was buried in a large complex with the huge Wake Forest football stadium, a coliseum, a fairgounds, and acres of other buildings. It had the look of an ampitheater: the grandstand was built into the side of a hill so fans walked down to their seats. The grandstand canopy was wood and, in another old-fashioned touch, a brick wall *à la* Wrigley Field ran behind home plate from first to third.

Motorboat's home run was his first of the year. Before spring training, he had been projected for assignment to Cincinnati's AA team in Chattanooga, but ended up in its Carolina League class A farm team. A native Alabaman, he had been in professional baseball since 1987, playing in rookie and class A leagues. He had speed, but hadn't hit with much authority. 1993 would prove to be a breakthrough year, at least at the class A level. By midseason, Motorboat had eighteen home runs and was hitting .330, figures good enough for a July call up to Chattanooga. Uncharacteristically, he had only six stolen bases for Winston-Salem when he was called up. Apparently Motorboat either ran *or* hit, but not both in the same season.

I was just as interested in Motorboat's nickname as in his developing skills, though. I kept a separate page in my notebook for gion. The team picture showed seventeen young men, including the manager, in flannel suits. Small rosters were common in that period at class D level. They carried five pitchers, two second basemen, two catchers, one player listed as "utility," and a manager who probably played in a pinch. At all other positions, the roster listed only one name. The team posed in the classic three-tier sitting-kneeling-standing formation. In the background, bleachers and the backs of several buildings hinted at the field on which they played. Since I was driving up Route 62 into Virginia anyway, I stopped off to see if the old park was still there.

Even on a Sunday afternoon the downtown Mount Airy area was busy. Andy Griffith had grown up in the town; several businesses referred to Mayberry or to one of the characters in the popular television series. It was one of the best examples I had seen in the South of how to keep a town alive. The stores had been recycled into specialty shops but had not folded up when core business activity had shifted to the strip on Route 62, over to the west of town.

The village movie theater now housed a visitor's center. The blue-green and white paint was faded and chipped, but it still looked much the same as when Andy got his first taste for the movies.

Inside, a woman stood behind the old concession stand, which now held pamphlets and posters instead of popcorn and Super Duds. She bore a striking resemblance, so help me, to Aunt Bee. When she told me she had grown up in Mount Airy, I asked if she remembered the old ballpark.

"I went to ball games there when I was a young girl," she said. "The town really supported the teams in those years right after the war." The park had been torn down, though, to make way for a police station.

The old theater, on the other hand, had remained practically untouched. Aunt Bee showed me the inside, seats still in place, and on the screen a mural that was continuously projected, of an idealistic, small town America. It was Mount Airy's past the way it is remembered but of course never was.

Mount Airy had recently been voted one of the one hundred best spots to retire in the United States, which will probably be its kiss

76

of death. Only the day before, Aunt Bee told me, Oprah Winfrey had been in town filming her television program there. The late afternoon sun was hazy and about ten miles to the northwest, the Blue Ridge Mountains gave off that azure glow for which they are named. Forty-five years ago, walking through the quaint streets to watch a ball game with the mountains as a backdrop must have been a very Mayberry kind of experience. Maybe they overdo the Andy Griffith shtick a little in Mount Airy, but there you can see what is still alive and positive in a small southern town. The 1948 Mount Airy Graniteers may have lost their ballpark, but their city has stood well against the second half of the twentieth century.

A full house at Texas League Park, c. 1950, during the golden age of minor league baseball. (Courtesy of Tulsa Drillers Baseball Club)

The Oiler Grill, located alongside the left-field line facing outside Texas League Park, in 1948. Patrons could drive in, order food, and listen to Tulsa Oiler away games while they ate. (Courtesy of Wayne McCombs, Claremore, OK)

Overhead view of Texas League Park, at Fifteenth and Sandusky, Tulsa, 1953. No game is in progress, but the Oiler Grill has a little business. (Courtesy of Wayne McCombs, Claremore, OK)

Sweetspot at a lunch stop in Georgia. A combination office, living space and reliable, smooth transportation.

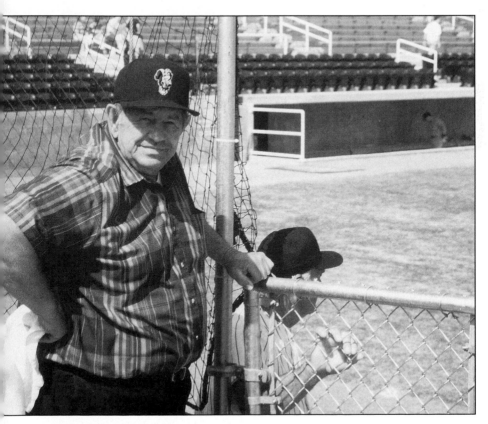

Paul Eames, for whom the park in Albany, GA, is named. Wally Moon is watching the action during batting practice.

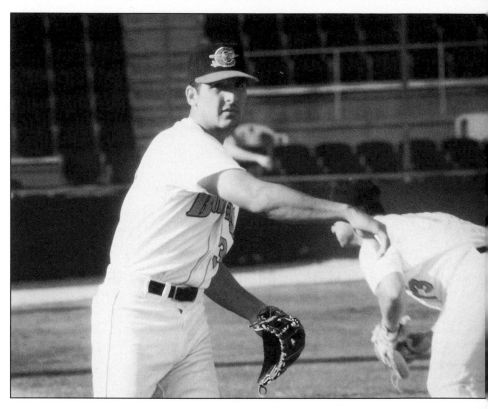

Jose Flores, shortstop for the Capital City Bombers , Columbia, SC.

World War Memorial Stadium, Greensboro, NC. One of the oldest diamonds in Dixie, built before world wars had numbers.

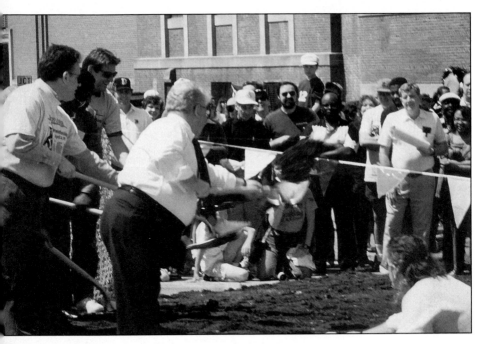

Groundbreaking for a new stadium in Durham, NC.

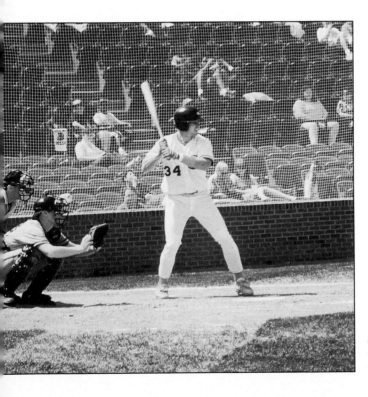

Waiting for the pitch, Ernie Shore Field, Winston-Salem, NC.

A police station now graces the field where the 1948 Mt. Airy Graniteers played. (Courtesy of David Beal, Mt. Airy, NC)

°1948 "GRANITEERS" - BLUE RIDGE LEAGUE.

1ST ROW — ZWELLING - 1ST B.; TEER - 2ND B.; TREECE - P, HOLMES - S.S., YEARICK - C.;
2ND ROW — MARSHALL - R.F.; WILLIAMS - R, SOLTERS - UTILITY, MIXON - R,
3RD ROW — HALL - C., HOLT - L.F, KING - P., DAVIS - 3RD.B., ESSIC - 2ND.B., AKINS C.F.
JACKSON - P., CASBIER - MANAGER.

Watt Powell Park, Charleston, WV. Railroad tracks beyond right field tempt left-handed hitters when a train rolls by.

Nashville's quirky Sulphur Dell, 1908, with Butler choking up on the bat. Note the dirt lane from home plate to the pitcher's mound. (Courtesy of National Baseball Library & Archive, Cooperstown, NY)

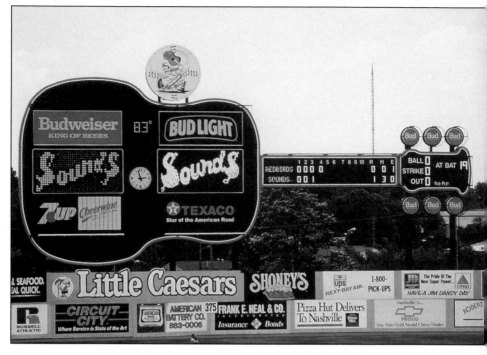

Scoreboard at Herschel Greer Stadium, Nashville, TN, paying homage to "Music City."

Artificial turf infield at Tim McCarver Field, Memphis, TN.

6

The Night the Lights
Went Out in Lynchburg

I PICKED UP THE BLUE RIDGE PARKWAY down near the North Carolina
border and drove along the spine of the Blue Ridge Mountains to
the Roanoke Valley in Virginia. The parkway connected the Shen-
andoah National Park in Virginia and the Great Smokey Mountains National Park in North Carolina and Tennessee. At high ele-
vations, the road gave a sensation of gliding along a mountain path.
Mountain laurel crowded the pavement and the white pines grew
close enough to form a canopy overhead. On a Monday morning, I
had the road almost to myself. It was not a commuter highway and
tourists came only on the weekends to look at the scenery.

As I dropped in elevation from three thousand feet to the valley
floor, which lay at about one thousand feet, the redbud maples
went from bare to new buds to full bloom, as if I were watching
time-lapse photography. The great valley, which contained the
Salem-Roanoke area, extended from New York to Alabama and
where I descended was bounded by the Alleghenies on the west and
the Blue Ridge Mountains on the east. In the springtime it was lush
and green. Tiny Salem, in the middle of the valley, had a team in
the Carolina League.

Municipal Field in Salem has enough idiosyncrasies to satisfy
even the most nostalgic baseball fan. I drove over to meet Sam
Lazarro, the Salem Buccaneers general manager, and to watch batting practice. The club offices were located upstairs from a karate

of the open press box to talk sports. Brian was sports editor for several weekly publications in the Salem-Roanoke area, and was a rich source of baseball information.

The evening got colder and colder. In the sixth inning, we looked down into the Buccaneers' bullpen and saw an open fire burning, with several pitchers warming their hands over the blaze. Sam Lazarro came into the press box a little later with the information that they were burning broken bats. He looked nervous because the fire was near the tarp used to cover the infield. He didn't make the players douse the blaze but continued to look warily toward the bullpen all during the game.

The Buccaneer pitchers had a few fires on the field to worry about, as well, as Durham worked them for thirteen hits and eleven runs. This barrage included four home runs and two triples. Despite the almost nonexistent power alleys, center field was deep (408 feet) and permitted frequent triples over the center fielder's head. Caroms off the cinderblock walls gave the outfielders fits, and the scoreboard, located only about 330 feet from home plate, suffered a broken bulb despite being covered with a net.

Rocky Bridges, employed by the Pirates as a roving infield instructor, was working with players during pregame warmups the following day. Rocky, a Texan who played eleven years in the majors during the fifties and early sixties, had celebrated his sixty-fourth birthday the week before. He was a popular figure in Salem, having managed the team a few years before. According to Sam Lazarro, he got mad only twice all year, both times because the beer wasn't in the clubhouse fast enough after games were over.

Rocky was the epitome of that much underappreciated role player, the utility infielder. In an era known for player stability with teams, he played for seven teams in eleven years. He had over four hundred at bats in only one of those years, but hung on with a .247 lifetime batting average and little home run power because he could play three infield positions. Now, despite having arthritis in his hands and, apparently, in his legs, Rocky traveled the Pirates' farm circuit hitting grounders to young infielders. I asked him about how fielding skills develop compared to hitting ability.

"Hitting skills actually develop earlier. I just look for glaring errors. Sometimes I come to work out something about a specific player." Rocky, at five feet eight inches tall and 170 pounds, talked around a mass of chewing tobacco that significantly increased his weight. He shot grounders out with precision, grunting slightly if one was a foot or two from its intended trajectory.

By game time that evening, conditions seemed perfect again. The temperature was in the sixties with no wind. At 7:00 P.M., the sun cast long shadows across the grass and the lights were on. Behind home plate I could smell the grass and the damp infield dirt. The Blue Ridge Mountains stood half in shadow, half in sunlight. By the fourth inning, however, the temperature had dropped again and I headed for the press box.

A plaque inside the ballpark at Salem contains a poignant message. Under a bronze relief of a ballplayer's head, it reads:

Dedicated to the Memory of
Francisco Alfredo Edmead
1956–1974

Who on August 22, 1974
was fatally injured during
a game played at Salem, Va.
United States, between the
Salem Pirates and the Rocky
Mount Phillies in the Class
A Carolina League.

He was one of the most
highly regarded players in
the Pirate organization and a
credit to the Dominican Republic,
but even more important, he
enjoyed the reputation of a
kind and decent human being.

I asked Brian Hoffman about the incident. It had happened during his first year as scorer with the club. Edmead, the right fielder, came in on a pop fly as the second baseman faded back on it. He dove for the ball and his head hit the second baseman's knee, which was covered by a metal brace. The right fielder crumpled and lost consciousness. He was rushed to the hospital, but later that evening, died. Unbeknownst to his team, Edmead had been born with a paper-thin skull, and what would have produced no more than a headache or a concussion in another player had been fatal to the young Dominican. No PA announcement was made, so that the manager could tell the players after the game was finished. His playing manager, Pablo Cruz, had been the second baseman involved in the collision.

Baseball parks, like persons, have personalities. You can get a feel for them, like meeting someone new, after a few hours, but deeper patterns and traits emerge slowly. Municipal Field had such a quirky personality that I couldn't imagine seeing a routine game there if I had stayed all summer. This one saw fifteen total runs with four home runs, three of which were really routine flies. Managers almost never ran anyone, because even the weakest hitter could lift a fly over those cozy walls.

I felt sorry for the pitchers. During the second game, a Salem pitcher sent word up to the press box that he thought a run scored the previous inning should be unearned. Occasionally, situations occur in a game in which the scorer's judgment determines whether a run is earned or unearned. In this case, an error allowed a runner to go to second on a single. The next batter doubled, and Brian ruled that the runner could have scored from first and therefore was the pitcher's responsibility. The pitcher had relayed a detailed message containing his viewpoint, and Brian was trying to evaluate it. "Can you see his point?" he asked everyone within earshot. While the debate was going on, the pitcher hung a curve and the batter hit it over the fence and off the roof of a house across the street. The press box erupted in laughter. "He should concentrate on the batter at the plate," Brian said. "One earned run doesn't mean a hell of a lot in this park."

Lynchburg, Virginia, is Falwell country. While cousin Jerry sees to the spiritual needs of folks in this city of seven hills, Calvin Falwell makes sure that baseball fans have a place to meet their needs for the American pastime. Calvin is president of the Lynchburg Baseball Corporation, which owns the Lynchburg Red Sox, a Bos-

ton affiliate. I sat through a shortened Carolina League contest between Lynchburg and the Winston-Salem Spirits with Calvin, his
wife, and his adult son Terry, who had been a batboy for the
Lynchburg team in his youth. Calvin is a distinguished-looking
gentleman who was honored for his contributions to Lynchburg
baseball in 1992 with a plaque, which now resides at City Stadium.

Falwells had lived for two hundred years on the same piece of
land in Lynchburg. Formerly a dairy farm, the property now
housed several businesses and had been annexed by the city. Calvin
Falwell first organized a group to buy a baseball franchise for
Lynchburg in the 1950s. His lifelong interest went back to boyhood
when his father drove a bus for prewar semipro baseball teams in
Lynchburg. Teams of that era played at the same location where
City Field was later built.

"In those days," Calvin told me, "people would drive to the field
and park their cars around where left field and the clubhouse are,
and watch games from their cars. Sometimes the afternoon sun
glancing off their windshields would blind the hitters, and the umpire would make them move their cars. And I saw at least two car
windows broken by line drives."

Calvin Falwell had always been a hands-on owner. In 1959, the
umpire ejected Lynchburg's manager from a game. There were no
other coaches so the players continued the game unmanaged. Unfortunately, a long-simmering cauldron of bad feeling over playing
time erupted and a free-for-all broke out among the Lynchburg
players. The bench emptied, as it were. The other team watched in
amazement as the Lynchburg players pummeled each other, and
waited for the melee to end so the game could continue. Falwell
and a police officer finally restored order and sat on the bench to
maintain tranquility for the rest of the game.

Lynchburg was without baseball in 1960 and 1961 but in 1962
events connected with civil rights unrest brought a team back for a
few games at the end of the season. Savannah had an entry in the
class AA South Atlantic League in 1962, and late in the season was
in a pennant race. But the racial tension in Savannah had become
potentially explosive. The franchise sought a new home to avoid

fans into Watt Powell the previous year, the second highest attendance in the South Atlantic League, despite having a small market and antiquated facilities. The concrete grandstand was cracked and had so many leaks that Dennis had to install indoor gutters to channel water when it rained. The national association had recently sent a letter threatening to revoke the franchise because the clubhouse, concessions, and handicapped access to the press box did not meet PBA standards. Dennis's other woes included perennial bad weather in the spring and having to share the field with the University of Charleston part of the year. "Charleston is better suited for a short-season league," Dennis admitted. "There isn't enough flat land in the Kanawha Valley to build a new park, and the place is too far gone to meet standards for class A."

According to Dennis, Watt Powell once had the largest dimensions of any professional park in the United States. Though baseball had been played on the site for most of the century, the present facility dated to 1948. The original dimensions were 360 feet down the left field line, 466 feet to left center, 527 feet to dead center, 528 feet to right center, and 330 feet to right. Present dimensions had been scaled back to 340 feet (left), 406 feet (center), and 330 feet (right). The power alleys were still an impressive 390 and 384 feet, however, and a sixteen-foot wall surrounded the immense green outfield. Dennis and I walked behind the present fence to see the old outer concrete wall, which was still in place. He told me that Ted Kluzewski had hit one over the old centerfield wall in an exhibition game. Given the height of the wall, the total distance would have to come close to six hundred feet. I said that I had never heard about this singular feat before. Dennis replied that he had heard the story from a reliable source, but he stopped short of vouching for its accuracy.

Dennis had a history of taking on down-and-almost-out baseball situations and turning them around. He started in 1979 in Gastonia, North Carolina (SAL), where he won a minor league executive of the year award. He moved to Macon, Georgia, and took over a team whose previous owners had skipped out on $85,000 worth of debts. Dennis repaid the debts and made $15,000 net profit. He moved to Spartansburg, South Carolina, next and revived an almost equally numb franchise. Dennis had often ended up having to undertake construction projects single-handedly, like building an office facility in Winston-Salem, his next stop, by himself. By then Dennis was an owner. While living in the locker room in Winston-Salem's park, Dennis married Lisa and acquired a partner in his baseball franchise masochism. In 1987, they moved over to the present situation in Charleston, West Virginia.

Dennis obviously was a marketing and sales virtuoso, but he upheld strict policies about advertising. I remarked that the familiar Marlboro man sign was missing. "I think it's ridiculous to talk about baseball and clean living and take money from cigarette and beer companies," he said. He showed me a large family seating area where smoking and drinking were prohibited. Such areas are not unusual in the minor leagues, but these seats had a prominent placement in Watt Powell Park.

Dennis began telling me about plans to field a AA team in Lexington, Kentucky, by 1995. It became apparent that a few things were still missing. Dennis didn't own a team to move to Lexington; Lexington didn't have a ballpark and hadn't made a commitment to build one; and Lexington hadn't sponsored professional baseball since 1954. For someone with less of a track record, these problems would have seemed insurmountable. For Dennis, they seemed almost matter of fact.

When Dennis excused himself to go spell Lisa in taking care of Wyatt, I walked onto the field. The groundskeeper was working on the batter's box. "You should get extra pay for an outfield that size," I suggested. He agreed. For all its size, however, Watt Powell looked like a hitter's park. I stood at home plate, looking over the center field fence at a large, heavily wooded hill punching up about three hundred feet and beginning about fifty yards beyond the fence. I could imagine a white, spinning spheroid coming out of the dark background and mentally made good contact. Just beyond the right-field wall, train tracks ran along a ten-foot elevation, and I could see the cars of a train from home plate. A left-handed hitter must feel a tangible temptation when a train chugs past because it seems reachable.

Later, the scorer told me that several balls had been hit into moving coal cars. I had read differently, that Rudy York and Luke Easter had come close but hadn't actually reached moving trains. The only case that was fairly well documented was that of a ball hit by Randy Bush of the Toledo Mud Hens of the International League on April 14, 1982. It landed on a moving coal train behind and above the right-field fence and was supposed to have traveled two hundred miles. I liked Watt Powell. In this ballpark, fact and fiction blended the way dusk became darkness.

During my Charleston sojourn, when I wasn't at Watt Powell I stayed at Kanawha State Forest, south of town. In April and May, by traveling north I had stayed in an extended spring, where the azaleas and dogwoods and redbuds were always in bloom. I backed Sweetspot into a small glen, ringed by wooded hills and serenaded by a small brook leading back into a dark hollow. Spring wild-flowers glittered in the bright sunshine. Their whimsical names—Dutchman's breeches, bloodroot, pink lady's slipper, jack-in-the-pulpit—had been assigned in simpler times, even before spring in Appalachia meant the beginning of another baseball season.

My second night at Watt Powell, the Wheelers brought in a relief pitcher named Pickett in the top of the third. He had just joined the team and was not listed in the media handouts. He immediately walked the bases full, then struck out two, then a batter reached on an error, and then they began to hit him. The immense power alleys were in shadow and the outfielders almost disappeared on balls hit into the gap. The lighting was the worst I saw on the trip. To add to Pickett's problems, the scorer was unusually generous in scoring dropped flies as base hits, probably because of the dim lighting.

Pickett then hit a batter, who had to leave the game for X rays. The next batter hit a double. Pickett's fastball was in the mid-eighties, but had little movement on it. He had a slow, roundhouse curve, which he used as a change-up, but had trouble getting it over. He was most successful when he was "sneaky fast." A moderately fast pitch would be followed by one with a slower motion but last-second follow-through made the pitch faster than the previous one. Unfortunately, they were hitting his setup pitch a mile.

Pickett was taken out in the top of the sixth. I was still marveling over the worst pitching performance I had seen in a long time, when the scorer announced his line in the press box. Despite walking five, giving up three doubles and a single, having one error committed behind him, hitting a batter, and allowing two long outs that would have been home runs almost anywhere else (including most major league parks), he had given up only two earned runs (plus three unearned) thanks to the timing of the error.

Unlike in life, things have a way of balancing out in baseball. A week and a half earlier, I had sympathized with pitchers as routine flies disappeared out of cozy Municipal Field in Salem, Virginia. Watt Powell Park had been a guardian angel for Pickett, but sooner or later he'll end up pitching in a park where the devil will get his due.

Before the season was over, I read in *Baseball America* that Dennis Bastien had acquired an option to buy the AA Southern League Nashville Xpress and planned to operate the team out of Lexington, Kentucky, in 1995. To do so, he traded in the class A Wheelers, in much the same way that other people trade in an old car on a new model. The owner of the Xpress planned to sell the Wheelers back to a local Charleston group, so Watt Powell will resound with the cracks of wooden bats for the foreseeable future.

Pete ("The Old Gladiator") Browning, who played baseball in Louisville, Kentucky, was one of the early tragic figures of the game. One day in 1884, he broke a bat (the least of his misfortunes) during a game attended by John Andrew Hillerich, who worked for his father in a woodworking shop in Louisville. The young man took Browning back to his father's shop, put a piece of white ash on a lathe, and turned it as Pete directed. Next day, Browning used his new bat, and had three hits. Not long afterward the Hillerichs decided that there was more money in bats than in butter churns.

Pete Browning had the reputation of being ignorant and illiterate. He gave his bats biblical names and thought that each one had only a certain number of hits in it. He was a good hitter, despite this eccentric thinking, and other players began to believe that he was onto something with the new Louisville bats. Unfortunately,

95

Pete also suggested that drinking helped him hit, and his beer consumption was legendary.

In truth, the Old Gladiator suffered from a condition called mastoiditis. The disease left him almost deaf, contributing to his appearance of stupidity, and probably eventually led to a brain infection. Drinking may not have helped him hit so much as to play through pain. After his baseball career, he was committed to an insane asylum and died at the early age of forty-four.

By the first part of the twentieth century, J. Frederick Hillerich and Sons were pioneering the concept of athletic endorsements. Honus Wagner was the first player to be paid for allowing his signature to be branded onto bats, followed by Larry Lajoie and Ty Cobb. Today about 70 percent of current major leaguers are under contract for bat signatures, and the company has eight thousand metal inscriptions (both past and present) in its files.

I had driven across Kentucky to see how bats are made. The first thing I learned was that the Louisville Slugger is made not in Louisville but across the Ohio River in Indiana. The huge production plant has 250,000 square feet (almost seven acres) under one roof. Inside, the noise level is high, but the wonderful smell of wood being worked permeates every corner and helps to compensate.

Bats are made from northern white ash harvested in New York and Pennsylvania. The company has tried hickory and hackberry, but ash is clearly the strongest wood. The trees have to be at least sixty years old before they are cut. After arriving at the plant, the wood is stored four to six weeks, until a 12 to 15 percent moisture content is achieved. The wood is weighed and graded three times on a scale of one to four. Only the highest grade is used for professional bats.

Semiautomatic lathes spin out a bat every fifteen seconds. One aspect of bat making has changed little since the days of Pete Browning. The trademark is still burn branded into the wood and then the wood is sanded to remove yellow scorch marks. In early stages, a peg or knob protrudes from the grip end of the bat for ease in turning and working. After branding, the bat goes through a finishing machine that removes the pegs, stamps numbers on the end and flame tempers the bat to make it darker.

Some bats then are mechanically hollowed out at the meat end to make them lighter without altering their length. This modification is legal according to the baseball community. Finally, the bat is hand dipped into clear lacquer and hung to dry for thirty minutes.

Hillerich and Bradsby, as the company is now called, is an integral part of baseball tradition, and is sensitive to its role as bat maker. While electronic lathes and tracer lathes partly automate the general production, some bats are still hand turned. If a persnickety player shows up with peculiar specifications, he can watch the same process Ty Cobb observed eighty years ago.

I asked a worker why players are always told to hold the bat with the trademark up. He said that the wood's strongest course was bound by the visible grain, running lengthwise under the trademark. The sweet spot produces greater power not only because of physics but because the wood is stronger there. Contact with that point, he added, produces a tenor sound instead of a toneless thunk.

Aluminum bats are made in the company's California plant. I asked my tour guide if she was aware that another company was making bats composed of plastic and sawdust. She said no, apparently truthfully, as the alarmed look on her face suggested that I had just ruined her day.

Before leaving the plant, I stopped at the souvenir counter to claim the custom bat I had ordered before my tour. It was a beautiful piece of white ash, 36 inches long, newly turned and lacquered, and had my name forever burned into the business end. I had vowed not to collect souvenirs on the trip, and this was the first item I had bought. Still, Sweetspot's cab was beginning to look like a teenager's bedroom. I had collected a few errant baseballs while watching batting practices, had been given a few caps, and had colorful press passes hanging from the visors and mirror. I walked out with my new bat to add to the collection, fondling it along the way.

Even apart from the manufacture of baseball's most famous bats, Louisville was closely connected to the early development of the game. The Ohio River city fielded teams in the American Association, an early big league rival of the National League, from 1882 through 1891, and for the 1892–1893 season was admitted into the senior circuit. One year the team nickname was the Night Riders, a reference to participants in Kentucky's tobacco raids of that period. The name probably didn't increase attendance by African-Americans, however, who were watchful of Klan activity around this southern city. Another label of questionable taste was applied to the 1890 team, which was called the Cyclones because a tornado hit Louisville in March of that year. The tornado had killed seventy-five persons.

For most of the early years of baseball, the game penetrated no farther south than the banks of the Potomac in the East. In the Midwest, the Ohio formed a similar barrier except for Louisville, which was just across the river. For all the seemingly long association of the South and baseball, the national pastime's beginnings were distinctly northern and eastern.

Baseball has actually had two beginnings, one dramatically invented and idealized, the other real and more evolutionary than revolutionary. Neither, however, had anything to do with the South. The mythical origin of baseball can be traced to the need to fit the national pastime into an American framework, and to believe that its origin came out of the fiber of the new nation. A commission was appointed in 1907 to fix, once and for all, the beginnings of baseball. Solely on the written testimony of one elderly respondent, the commission accepted the idea that Abner Doubleday had laid out the game in its essentials in 1839, in Cooperstown, New York. Note that the witness, a Mr. Abner Graves, was recalling events of sixty-eight years before. General Doubleday himself never mentioned baseball as one of his interests. His childhood interests seem to have been mapmaking and reading, and the critical events of his adult years included four years spent getting the southern rebels back in line during the Civil War.

In the early twentieth century, when the commission met, sentiment against immigration was peaking. Earlier immigrants from northern and western Europe had blended rather easily into the new nation. Feelings were turning against the new immigrants from southern and eastern Europe who were streaming through Ellis Island with foreign languages, religions, and customs, because they were assimilating slowly. This sentiment, which broadened to a general antiforeign, nationalistic fervor, would peak in 1920 with the adoption of restrictive immigration quotas to slow the torrent to a trickle. To imagine baseball, the most American game, as having a foreign origin became unthinkable. Besides, anyone who has ever been to the quaint village of Cooperstown, New York, can easily see that baseball *should* have been invented there, whether it was or not.

Baseball's true origins have been traced most convincingly by Harold Seymour in *Baseball: The Early Years*, a thorough if somewhat grouchy review of the game's roots. Baseball developed from the English game of rounders. Published accounts show that rules for the two games were the same until 1829, and gradually began to diverge. The term "base-ball" was published in a rhyme as early as 1744 in England, and the journal account of a revolutionary soldier in 1778 reveals that games of "base" were played at Valley Forge. No doubt, other antecedents of the game can be found in other cultures, because the game simply evolved as an organized means of having fun with a stick or club and something that was round and could roll or fly through the air. Games played in early nineteenth-century America included barn ball, where one boy would throw the ball against a barn and another boy would bat it; and "one old cat," in which one boy would throw to a batter, who would hit the ball, run to a designated point, and try to return to the base before the second boy could field the fall and "soak" the runner, or plunk him, with the ball. As settled areas became more dense in the northeast, the games became more elaborate, and two, three, and four old cat were born. As players were added, rules became more fixed and extensive as needed.

If a single frozen instant and a solitary creator is needed against which to mark time and celebrate baseball's birth, the year 1846 and the name Alexander Cartwright are the logical candidates. Beginning in 1842, a group of New York gentlemen had been meeting to play baseball. Rival teams would meet irregularly at a vacant lot in Manhattan near Madison Avenue and Twenty-seventh Street. Cartwright, a bank teller and volunteer fireman, eventually sugbegan and baseball had to take a back seat until political issues could be settled.

The popular view has been that Union soldiers who ended up in Confederate prisoner of war camps, as a means of filling up leisure time and providing discipline and exercise, demonstrated the game to their southern captors, who then spread the essentials around after hostilities ceased. No doubt awareness of the game expanded through such contact, as did other aspects of northern culture. One wartime game, played on Christmas Day in 1862, featuring a team from the 165th New York who picked nine players from other Union regiments in Hilton Head, South Carolina, was witnessed by forty thousand spectators. Records show, nonetheless, that southern soldiers played baseball among themselves during the war. Baseball "artists" from New Orleans may have had as much or more to do with spreading the game to other Confederate soldiers as did northern soldiers. Al Spalding, the pioneer pitcher whose name lives on in sports equipment, wrote an early history of baseball in 1911. He repeated stories about a series supposedly held between Union and Confederate troops when hostilities were in abeyance before the campaign leading to Richmond. While Spalding could not find anyone who had played in these matches forty-five years earlier, other contests such as horse races were held between opposing forces during lulls in the war and the story of a baseball series is at least plausible.

The war may have temporarily slowed the growth of baseball, but that is all. Postwar baseball clubs began to show up in the South, many predictably named after Confederate war heroes. Norfolk fielded a team called the Stonewalls in 1866, and continuing the bad luck of the Confederates during the recent unpleasantness, they lost their first game 65 to 19. Washington, D.C., still had the National Base Ball Club, which used the Mall as their playing field. Unlike the hapless twentieth-century Senators, the amateur Nationals were a powerhouse. In 1867, they made a road trip west and played in Louisville, another fringe southern town, and in St. Louis, but had to report that the "western" teams weren't much of a match. The Nationals beat St. Louis 113 to 26.

In the late 1860s, a second team called the Mutuals emerged in

Washington, D.C. This team had rooms at the Willard Hotel and elected President Johnson an honorary member of the club. President Johnson returned the compliment by inviting members of the club to the White House. Interestingly, in his remarks to the team, the president said that he had played baseball as a youth, which would have been in the 1820s or even earlier.

By 1868, teams had begun forming not only in the larger southern cities, but in smaller ones also. Wetumpka and Prattsville in Alabama formed their first teams that year, and Pennsacola, Florida, fielded the Seminoles. As baseball spread throughout the South, however, changes in the northern sport were occurring that would have pervasive and long-term effects.

Baseball's umbrella organization in the formative years of amateur clubs was the National Association. In 1868, the organization for the first time recognized professionals. The following year, the famous Cincinnati Red Stockings, the team of all paid professionals, toured the nation and swept to an undefeated season with but one tie. The excitement generated by the superior play of the professionals reversed baseball's direction. Amateurs withdrew from the association during the spring of 1871 to form their own organization and, thereafter, amateur clubs soon ceased to be of any importance on a national level.

Beginning in the decade of the 1870s, the South began to attract the interest of northern baseball clubs because of warmer weather earlier in the season and preseason. In 1871, the Chicago White Stockings went to New Orleans in March to play the Lone Stars, the Southerners, and the Robert E. Lees. They beat the Lone Stars by a score of only nine to six. The Mutuals played exhibition games in the vicinity of Charleston and Savannah that same year, trips that could be seen as precursors of spring training. In 1888, the Washington club became the first team to train in Florida in the spring. The amateur Savannah club visited New York and New England in August of 1871, losing all their matches badly to northern amateur clubs. This was, however, the first time a club from the Deep South traveled north.

While baseball obviously had a foothold in the South before 1876, the activity was a drop in the bucket compared to that in the

North. Why was baseball so slow to develop in the South? The Civil War allowed as much opportunity for the learning and spread of baseball enthusiasm for southern soldiers as for northerners. Reconstruction was a hindrance, to put it mildly, but in the North, baseball had grown out of infancy and had supplanted contending games such as cricket as the national preference some time before the Civil War and its aftermath left the South in chaos.

The sparse population of the South helped keep baseball from developing quickly there. In *Cotton Fields and Skyscrapers*, David Goldfield establishes that in 1860, only New Orleans among leading southern cities had a population greater than one hundred thousand. Not coincidentally, New Orleans was the leading baseball city in the antebellum south. Only the development of cities made the growth of baseball possible. One of the many paradoxes about baseball is that agrarian society didn't allow baseball to develop, yet its dominant images are bucolic, and much of the argot has rural, not urban, origins. Players stand in the field, pitchers warm up in the bullpen, runners slide in the dirt, while flies are chased on the grass, and batters try to pummel the old horsehide (which, since 1974, has been a cowhide). As if to consciously reinforce the superiority of urban baseball, players are seasoned on the farm and called up to the big show in the cities when their skills are well-honed.

In the agrarian South, traditional outdoor pursuits such as hunting, fishing, and horse racing remained possible long after they had ceased to be practical in or near places like New York and Boston. Furthermore, the plantation-owning aristocracy in the South set the trends in leisure activity and favored established sports such as fox hunting. These trendsetters were slow to relinquish traditional pursuits and reluctant to allow a new, vulgar sport such as baseball a foothold.

The more rapid growth of baseball in the North was also aligned with industrialization, which was underway in the North at least two generations before it had a significant impact on the South. Baseball's growth in popularity at a national level depended upon the railroad to transport players across city, state, and regional boundaries. The first "tour" by the Excelsiors predated the Civil

War in 1860 and included various locations in New York and the mid-Atlantic states of Pennsylvania, Maryland, and Delaware. The South lagged behind not only in concentration of population to develop players and audiences, but in railroad transportation to make such team tours possible.

A second way industrialization was linked to early baseball was explained by Warren Goldstein in *Playing for Keeps: A History of Early Baseball.* The agrarian society needed generalists, people who could do many things well on the farm. Industry demanded specialists who could contribute a single specific mastered skill toward total product output. At first, baseball players were generalists but as the industrial revolution proceeded, so did specialization in baseball. No longer could one person master all the skills necessary on a ball field. The more agrarian South did not provide the reinforcement for specialization that was present in the North. Gradually, too, the work ethic of an industrial society began to be mirrored in baseball's paid performers. They were called "players" but expectations grew for practice, punctuality, commitment, in short, the same attributes that constitute productive work in an industrial society. A final link between industrialization and baseball was that factories forced a concentration of population for their workforces, and this also provided an audience for leisure activities.

One reason for baseball's growth in appeal was that it bridged a cultural gap between the middle and lower socioeconomic classes. Among the masses, baseball was a step up from cruder sports such as prizefighting; and among the genteel middle classes, it slowly was embraced and became a democratizing sport. Thus, in the North it provided an acceptable meeting ground for separate socioeconomic layers. In the antebellum South, the division between wealthy landowners and poor tenants was too wide for any sport to bridge.

Despite a long and storied history in the national pastime, Louisville had fallen victim to the minor league baseball torpor of the late 1960s and finally lost its team after the 1972 season. In 1982, the city renovated its stadium, attracted a AAA franchise, and began setting attendance records. Before the Buffalo Bisons regularly began drawing over one million fans in the late 1980s, the Louisville Redbirds were the perennial minor league attendance leader. Today, when all-time minor league attendance years are listed, Louisville holds six of the top twelve attendance years.

After seeing the petite ballparks of the southeastern class A clubs, I thought Cardinal Stadium in Louisville looked immense. The field had artificial turf and the outfield walls were painted blue with no signs. Three umpires, rather than the customary two, patrolled the field. Everything had a plastic, artificial look. The staff was formal and had bureaucratic procedures for entry and seating. This was big city baseball, at least for me. I had grown used to organizations where after a few days I knew most of the staff and people would come up and introduce themselves.

On the field, the game was played at a noticeably higher level. Dimensions were 360 feet to left, 405 feet to center, and 312 feet to right. The short right-field wall was made more difficult to reach with a barrier about sixteen feet high, which slanted backwards at eight feet and then rose vertically again. Hitters were strong enough to reach the distant walls (I saw six home runs, one over the center field fence) and many had big league experience. In the top of the third, the Redbird first baseman made a defensive marvel of a play on a ground smash to his left. He dove, backhanded the ball in midair, rolled, and released to the pitcher in one fluid, perfectly executed sequence of connected motions.

After the bottom of the sixth, Louisville had scored in every inning. Finally, in the bottom of the seventh, they were shut down, but only after a Redbird batter missed a home run by pulling it down the right field line fifteen feet foul. They eventually won 12–5.

Another difference at the triple AAA level was in entertainment; if Redbird Stadium was typical, the mascot was much more of a performer than at the class A level. Billy Bird raced out in a variety of small vehicles between innings, roaring down the foul lines and careening around the warning track. The athletic entertainer finally catapulted over the center field fence in a display of timing and daring that awed the large Friday evening crowd.

Next morning, I took out my well-used *Baseball America Direc-*

tory to check the minor league schedules. I could either stay in Louisville and watch balls take predictable hops on the artificial surface or drive eight hours to the southeast and then work my way back to the middle South. The choice wasn't difficult.

I took US 150 south and east to hook up with US 25, which shoots the gap at Cumberland and cuts off the eastern wedge of Tennessee. Interstates took me across the mountainous western tip of North Carolina. My luck with spring weather ran out in Greenville, South Carolina. On Sunday morning, it was hot and humid. The leaves were fully out, and summer had definitely arrived. I put a new supply of Dr. Pepper in my front seat cooler.

I drove out to Greenville Municipal Stadium before noon to see the Braves, an Atlanta AA farm club, work out before playing a Sunday afternoon game. The stadium was built in 1984 just for baseball, which is indicated by how the grandstand curves uniformly down the foul lines. As a member of the class AA Southern League in 1992, Greenville accomplished the almost impossible feat of winning one hundred games. For a modern minor league team to win this many games, it had to play at a .700 pace over 142 games (Greenville actually played 143 regular season games and ended up at .699). In addition to the usual obstacles of injuries, slumps, and probability ("you win a third and lose a third just by taking the field; it's what you do with the other third that counts"), minor league teams have to contend with call-ups. Players who get hot at bat or on the mound were often called up to the next higher level. Almost automatically, an exceptionally good team that loses a few of its dominant players regresses in the standings. The Braves had not only ruled the Southern League all season (Chattanooga had won ninety games and finished ten games out) but had won six more in postseason play.

Almost all the 1992 Greenville Braves who played regularly had been promoted to Atlanta's AAA farm club at Richmond in 1993. Yet, the 1993 Braves were at 20–10 going into the Sunday afternoon game and were being subjected to the inevitable comparisons with last year's powerhouse. I talked briefly with Bruce Kimm, Greenville's first-year manager, before he picked up a bat to go to

107

work. The coaches were working on situational hitting that after-noon. For example, runners were stationed on first and began mov-ing toward second before the pitch. Batters practiced hitting the hole when the infielders shifted to cover bases. Other situations were called out by the batting practice pitcher—infield back, infield in, squeeze on, runner on third, one out, run and hit—and batters altered stances and hand positions on the bat accordingly.

Bruce, a forty-one-year-old former major league catcher, began hitting line drives to outfielders playing shallow. I was fascinated to hear him use an infinite number of inflections and four-letter words to convey different meanings. Often the exclamation would be accompanied by a wave of the bat or an arm to further accentu-ate the message. Remarkably, outfielders would nod to assure him that the terse point had been decoded.

"Bleep!" (Sorry, I meant to hit that one more to your left.)

"Bleep!" (You're right, I shouldn't have short-hopped you when we were working on your throw to third.)

"Bleep!" (I don't know why, but I got under that one too much and sent it over your head.)

The Sunday afternoon crowd was sparse, perhaps because it was hot and there was no shade. Anyone who builds a baseball park without a roof should have to spend eternity sitting in the sun in hazy, humid, hot weather. Many fans put programs over their heads to shield themselves from the sun. On the field, Greenville looked like a very mortal baseball team. The Birmingham Barons beat them 8–2.

The first night in Greenville, I stayed in a state park outside of town. Next day I drove into town to do some chores and see how a night in an air-conditioned motel would feel. Before leaving on the trip, one my most irrational and useless worries concerned getting my laundry done. Because I had never used laundromats, I had no knowledge of how they operated. My fears had me believing that these were dangerous places where a variety of crimes occurred regularly. I supposed that drug deals were made there routinely, that rapes occurred in them a few times each week, and that almost daily a gunman would drop by to rob the attendant of change from the machines. Like other images I concocted about places I had never seen, my fantasies were way off the mark.

I found instead that they were clean, well-managed places which were frequented by congenial people. Laundromats have several social functions beyond simply being places to wash and dry clothes. Patrons socialize, share information, and even share problems in what becomes an impromptu emotional support group. Men hit on women and women on men while their clothes are agitated; and everyone cheerfully dispenses advice to novices on working the machines.

Once I was waiting for a dryer to finish its cycle, watching the big glass fronted cylinder rotate and tumble my clothes, and overheard an exchange between two women who were folding laundry behind me. "You can always tell people who don't come here much," one said. "They watch their clothes go around."

Washing my clothes in a laundromat in Greenville, I made friends with the attendant. James Edward Brown was a trim, dapper, middle-aged black man. We spent an hour in conversation, and I told him about my trip and a little of my background. When the subject of race relations in the South came up, he was willing and even eager to discuss the issues. This was a departure from the usual; most southerners, black and white, dodged the topic when I tried to include it in conversation. James, I learned, was a former civil rights activist. He graduated from South Carolina State College in 1959 and went through the period of sit-ins, freedom rides, and other protests when the movement was dangerous, exciting, and optimistic. His complaint today isn't that things are headed in the wrong direction, just that nothing is happening. "CORE, SNCC, even the Black Panthers, are just names today, they don't do anything," he said.

As I was preparing to leave, James presented me a novel that he had written. A story about civil rights activists, it is called *The Plan*. Drafted while he was a junior in college, it was published a few years later by Vantage Press. On the back dustcover a young James Brown, dressed in an open shirt with its collar spilling onto a leisure suit jacket, looks out sensitively at the reader. James told me that he and others had tried to put some of the principles of

The Plan into practice in Greenville, but that reality had been more complicated than fiction.

After watching Greenville lose two games, I drove back into North Carolina to visit my niece in Brevard. After dinner, we drove over to her father's house. Buddy, my sister's former husband, lives in a house surrounded by huge trees on a quiet street. We all sat in the back yard, drank beer and watched my grand-nephew and grand-nieces play.

Buddy and his family typify small-town southern life. He lives, and will die, a few blocks from where he was born. His mother lives in a house across the back yard fence, and while we sat talking, other relatives came and went during the evening. Buddy works in a plant that makes machines for the textile industry, and has a ten-minute drive to work with no traffic. He fishes the lakes and rivers around Brevard on the weekends with his fishing partner, a man called Turkey. Their center of social life is the American Legion in Brevard, which until recently was the only place in town where you could drink alcohol on the premises. Buddy told me about a wild river near Brevard, and promised to take me there if I would stay until the weekend. It was so isolated, he said, that some of the holes may never have been fished.

I was tempted but passed up Buddy's offers to spend the night and stay longer and drove north, into the Pisgah Forest, parking Sweetspot a few feet from a trout stream. At first light, I got down to business, fishing a half mile of the stream before walking back down the road to make coffee.

When Crash Davis was cut from the Durham Bulls in the film *Bull Durham*, he hooked up with the Asheville Tourists in the South Atlantic League. There, Crash hit his minor league record-breaking home run and retired from baseball. A small part of the film was shot at famous old McCormick Field. Those who want to see the place now would be advised to pick up a copy of that film, because the old park is no more. I arrived in Asheville two years too late.

McCormick Field's formal opening was on April 3, 1924, and Ty

Cobb played in an exhibition game for the Detroit Tigers that day. The field had been named for Dr. Lewis M. McCormick, an early bacteriologist in Asheville, who sent flyswatter sales soaring by inaugurating the "Swat That Fly" movement in 1905.

The original McCormick had been one of the last wooden grandstand parks still in use. Many of baseball's hallowed names appeared there as minor leaguers or in exhibition games, including Babe Ruth. In 1931, the Babe looked out at the picturesque scene of this park etched into a wooded hillside and called it the most beautiful place to play in America. The reason he hadn't said this on an earlier visit in 1925 is that he hadn't made it from the train station to the park. The Babe collapsed on the platform and was hospitalized from, officially, eating too many hot dogs.

Two years ago McCormick was razed and rebuilt on the same plot of ground. The new ballpark lacks the historical character of its predecessor, but is nonetheless a captivating structure. The facade is red brick with a postmodern design, and seating takes the shape of an L, with the shank running from home plate down the right field line. A three-foot-high red brick wall surrounds the playing field. The sizeable grandstand roof is cantilevered with a small concrete press box, shaped something like a New England diner, perched on top of the stands. Dimensions are 328 feet to left, 406 feet to center, and a short 300 feet to right. In right field, a thirty-five-foot-high fence towers over the playing area. Fenway's green monster is only two feet higher.

"It's the highest fence in the minors," Ron McKee, the Tourists' general manager told me, "but that shows you how smart I am. If I had gone just three feet higher, I'd have had the highest fence in baseball."

Ron was beginning his fourteenth season as general manager in Asheville. Rotund and energetic, he is known for a personal approach to baseball management where fans are treated like family. It had been raining the afternoon I arrived in Asheville, and Ron was debating whether to leave the tarp on the field or take it off. He was wearing shorts, an old tee shirt, and sneakers. Four of the staff were discussing the situation, and collectively had three different opinions, including one strange proposal to roll it up halfway.

111

Two institutions in the heart of Nashville endeared me to the place. Across the plaza at the foot of Broadway on the river sat a square, unimpressive building that looked like an overgrown hot dog stand. The type of place usually hidden from tourists and known to locals only through word of mouth, Jack's Bar-B-Que was square in our path. Jack's sold mainly beer and food to go, but had a few tables with umbrellas on the sidewalk for "patio dining." While Tennessee pork shoulder is the traditional barbecue meat, Jack's also serves barbecued beef brisket Texas style. The story is that when Tennessean Sam Houston and his followers went to Texas to help out at the Alamo, they found that there were more cattle in Texas than hogs, and invented barbecued beef.

Jack dug a pit in 1976 and has been cooking on location and serving from pit to plate ever since. I had never been a booster of barbecued beef, but after trying both, found that Jack's beef was superior to his barbecued pork. And at Jack's, I learned about the Bohannon Brewery.

Brown bottles of Bohannon's Market Street Beer stood upright in a barrel of ice at Jack's. The taste was distinctive, mellow, and prominent enough to challenge the barbecue sauce. Before leaving Nashville on Monday morning, I walked to the brewery on Second Street (formerly Market Street). Although the business has only been open for a couple of years, the building dates from 1888 and is built on the site of Nashville's first brewery. The walls are bare brick, and visitors can look down on the beer-making process through windows. Inside the fermenting tanks barley, hops, yeast, and water combine to do their work. The high-ceiling interior is dim and the place smells, appropriately, like a brewery. I left carrying two mixed cases containing pilsner, golden ale, and the flavorful wheat beer, bucking them up Market Street to where Sweetspot was parked.

On Sunday, I convinced Zena that she should accompany me to a baseball game and see how I was spending my summer. In Nashville, baseball is played at Greer Stadium, away from downtown just off an interstate highway. The park occupies the site of the last great battle of the Civil War, at Fort Negley. Built in 1978, the park is symmetrical (330 feet to the lines, 405 feet to center) and has a seating capacity of sixteen thousand. Greer is home to the Nashville Sounds, a AAA club in the American Association, and in 1993, also hosted the Nashville Xpress, a AA team in the Southern League. Seating is in a circular, single-deck configuration with higher seats located a long distance from the field, as minor league parks go. A row of skyboxes sits atop the grandstand's back wall, and are in turn topped by a large press box. The most unusual feature of the park is a scoreboard in the shape of a guitar, paying homage to "Music City."

Nashville has gone from having one of the most absurd baseball parks in history to having one of the most ordinary. Sulpher Dell, where baseball was played from 1885 through 1963, was located downtown just 440 yards off the Cumberland River. The site was named for a sulphur spring and salt lick that had lured buffalo, then buffalo hunters, and finally white settlers. Teams played down below a bluff in a hole that was neither level nor big enough. No matter how it was configured, a short fence had to exist somewhere. For most of its history, left field was 334 feet, center field 421 feet, and right, a snug 262 feet. Right field was not only close in, but had an incline that began behind first base gradually, increased to a forty-five degree angle in shallow left, leveled off to a shelf about a third of the way up, and then continued at a forty-five degree angle to the fence. Right fielders played on the terrace and had to catch balls running uphill, downhill, and crosshill. Even putting a thirty-foot screen on top of the sixteen foot wooden fence in right didn't stop left-handed batters from dropping cheap home runs over the barrier.

Sulpher Dell was near the city dump and when the river overflowed in the spring, it carried odors into the ballpark. Outfielders, nearest to the dump, called the park "suffer hell." In 1954, Bob Lennon, a left-hander, hit sixty-four home runs for the Southern Association Nashville Volunteers. In a seventeen-year-long minor league career played almost entirely in other parks, Bob's second highest total was thirty-one home runs. In Southern Association history (Nashville belonged to this league during most of Sulpher Dell's existence), there were eight players who hit forty or more home runs in a season. Every one of them was a left-handed batter playing for Nashville. The miracle is that Nashville batters don't have all the minor league, single-season home run records before 1963, when the old park was last used.

Today's Southern League is a double A coalition with ten teams. The eastern division consists of the Carolina Mudcats in Zebulon, North Carolina, two Florida entries—Orlando and Jacksonville—Greenville, South Carolina, and Knoxville, Tennessee. In the western division, Alabama has two entries (Birmingham and Huntsville) and Tennessee has three (Memphis, Chattanooga, and Nashville). The league goes back to 1885 with an erratic beginning that stabilized in 1902. In its best-known incarnation it was called the Southern Association and included most of the larger southern cities. Atlanta, Little Rock, Mobile, and New Orleans were traditional members.

Transition from the Southern Association to the current Southern League was roundabout. In the early 1960s, the times caught up with baseball in Dixie. All the usual forces were at work—television kept fans at home, air-conditioning made hot southern nights at the ballpark less appealing, and interest in professional football was increasing—but the Southern Association had additional problems. The National League had taken Atlanta in 1962, and that city had been one of the league's mainstays. A more deep-rooted concern was the racial unrest of the period. The lunch room sit-ins had begun in 1961. Freedom rides and the civil rights efforts of Martin Luther King, Jr., created turmoil in southern cities, and ballparks were potential centers of racial confrontation. Baseball integrated after Jackie Robinson, and by the early sixties, only the class D Alabama-Florida League remained all white. Teams still had difficulty finding housing for black players, however, and chaotic events in the larger southern society funneled down into the diamonds of Dixie.

Under these conditions, the old Southern Association folded after 1961. In 1964, the South Atlantic League changed its name to the Southern League. Over the next three decades, the league slowly slipped many of the traditional old cities of the South back into the fold. Today, Birmingham, Nashville, Chattanooga, and Memphis once again form the backbone of Dixieball.

Zena left Nashville late Sunday night after we made plans to meet in New Orleans in a few weeks. "Maybe we can catch a ballgame there," I suggested, and got a noncommittal smile in return.

Monday morning I set up an appointment with the owner of the Nashville Sounds. No one could poke around minor league baseball for long without hearing about Larry Schmittou. He is the primary owner of the Nashville Sounds (American Association), the Huntsville Stars (Southern League), and the class A Winston-Salem Spirits (Carolina League). Lists of almost all National Association committees contain his name, and in 1993, he undertook an unusual experiment in operating a class AA Southern League team (the Nashville Xpress) in the same city and ballpark as his AAA team, the Sounds.

I was eager to find out how the novel situation was developing. Larry, who insisted on making our meeting a standard interview, had obviously answered the same questions many times before and seemed a little defensive.

"How did the Nashville Xpress get its name?" I asked.

"My son Ron came up with it. All the minor league ballparks used to have railroad tracks running just outside and many still do. It evokes that past, and we already had one team tying into the city's music industry [the Nashville Sounds]."

Larry told me that his ownership group had signed a contract to manage and operate the AA team that had been in Charlotte, North Carolina, the year before. Charlotte had received an expansion AAA franchise and the league wasn't able to place the AA team in a suitable southern city. The arrangement put two teams in one ballpark, with one staff, under Schmittou's control for a season.

"Problems?" I asked. Larry minimized the problems, saying that the field naturally required a little extra maintenance and of course the staff had to work harder to keep the place clean and dispense concessions with only seven days off during the season.

Sensing that the interview was almost over, I sprung my most abrasive questions last. "Has anyone suggested that there may be a conflict of interest in the situation, considering that you own the Huntsville team in the same league?"

Larry, sitting behind his large desk, folded his arms across his she had walked through an old cemetery in Dalton and had seen the Green family name on several tombstones. The note was a quarter-century old, but I drove to the corners of Stone and Happy Streets to check out the markers. The small cemetery covered about half a city block in an old section of Dalton. It was filled with oak trees. About half of the ground was mowed and the other half was overgrown. Many of the grave stones had tumbled over and were scattered around. Some had been nudged from below by roots of trees. A majority of the stones were marble and had been eroded beyond the point where names could be recognized. I saw a groundhog scurry under one headstone, which was lying flat on the ground, into a hole it had dug there.

I realized that I wasn't going to find out where Isham and Rebecca were buried, and in all likelihood I would be the last person to ever try. I knew all I ever would about my great-grandparents. I knew that marble tombstones and shotgun houses don't last forever, and that young boys should listen more carefully when a grandparent tells war stories.

JoLynn Drake, public relations manager for the Chattanooga Lookouts AA Southern League team, took me up to the roof of Joe Engel Stadium so I could take some panoramic pictures of the old ballpark. A recent graduate of the University of Florida in sport science, she had been with the team since the previous October. As usual in minor league baseball administration jobs, her work ranged over a diverse set of duties, including the production of publications and media relations. JoLynn was pretty in the way that only young southern women sometimes are, with a wholesome smile and an athlete's movements. She had played baseball on organized teams with boys and was totally devoted to the game. Her goal, she told me, was to be the first female general manager in the majors. If staying focused can accomplish that aim, JoLynn should have a good shot at it. A few nights later in the press box, a staff member was talking about another of his hard-working colleagues with disbelief:

"He didn't have to work! He could have been out on this really hot date! He'd rather be here at the park!"

"Who wouldn't?" asked JoLynn.

JoLynn didn't seem to be in a big hurry so we stayed on the roof and talked about baseball in Chattanooga. Joe Engel Stadium had all the credentials of a great ballpark. In 1930, Babe Ruth christened the park with its first home run in an exhibition game, one of many the Babe opened with a blast. The park and the neighborhood surrounding it had both grown old. Outside the right-field fence, railroad tracks held train boxcars sitting on sidings. Railyard sounds and clanging bells floated in on the warm afternoon breeze. Beyond right center, I could see a rusting steel bridge superstructure. After dark a stream of automobile headlights and taillights traced patterns of illumination across the bridge.

To the southwest, a neighborhood of older homes hinted that once a middle-class population had surrounded the old park, but economic decline was now evident. Across the street, outside the left-field fence, a fast-food restaurant had become a target for batting practice home runs. Its green plastic mansard roof sported several noticeable dents from balls that carried the street.

Despite its age, Joe Engel was exceptionally clean and modern looking. The exterior was pinkish brick with muted green roofing. Steel girders supported the roof canopy, which ran from first to third base. A modern press box sat atop the roof and offered an excellent view of the field. One of the few minuses in this fine park was that the grandstand was inclined at a very shallow angle, so fans behind the box seats were a long way from the action for a minor league park.

The groundskeeper told me that the field had been recently redone by a firm called Southern Turf. This company had been getting major contracts lately, surfacing fields and offering supervision for maintenance of its work afterward. It had taken the infield down two feet, and installed three miles of pipe under the playing surface. In 1990 and 1991, twenty-four rainouts had been called at Engel. In 1992, after installation of the new drainage system, that number had been reduced to one. The field looked a little ragged now in late May because the rye grass was dying and the bermuda hadn't fully taken hold.

When Engel opened in 1930, left field was 368 feet, left center

10

Deep in Dixie

LARRY FLEMING HAD RECOMMENDED Interstate 59 as a little-traveled and attractive line to Birmingham, Alabama. Before driving into Birmingham, I intended to stop in the small town of Trussville, Alabama, about twenty miles to the northeast, to talk with Jimmy Bragan, president of the Southern League. When I telephoned from the main street of the small town, Jimmy's wife Sarah told me that he had been held up in a meeting in Birmingham and wouldn't be available for awhile. Chancing upon a familiar candystriped revolving symbol, I used the time to visit a southern institution that I hadn't frequented in many years, the village barbershop.

The barber, who told me his name was Cecil, had the Chicago Cubs game on in the empty shop. Cecil obviously didn't keep an appointment book; a sign warned customers, "If you leave the shop, you lose your place in line." The Cubs game was a slow affair, so Cecil began filling me in on local color. Jimmy Bragan was a customer of his, and Jimmy, he said, knew the difference between barbering and what they do at salons.

"What," I asked, "is the difference?"

"They don't know anything about barbering, is the difference. Oh, they can cut your hair, make you look good, but that's not barbering. That's not barbering at all."

One difference was the way Cecil shaved my neck, using a hot cloth and shaving lather. Another was that I left with practically no hair at all. His haircut took care of me for the rest of the trip, and then some. The real difference, however, was gender. Cecil's washboards, cowbells, and spoons, billed itself as a Confederate band, and refused to go on without the uniforms. A month earlier, it had broken tradition and agreed to do a performance without playing "Dixie," staying instead with the traditional favorites "Oh! Susanna," "Sewanee River," and "When Johnnie Comes Marching Home."

In Mississippi, the NAACP had filed a lawsuit attacking the state flag as unconstitutional. As in Georgia, the state flag had an image of the "stars and bars" symbol of the Confederacy embedded in it, so both states faced a somewhat different dilemma than did Alabama. In talking with residents of all the Deep South states about the issue of Confederacy symbolism, whether in the form of flags, uniforms, or song, I could see an argument that was becoming increasingly heated.

Those who defended the display of Confederate symbols evoked the issue of pride. Ancestors had fought and died for the principles they believed in. The symbols represented history, warts and all. Freedom of expression gave everyone the right to display the Confederate symbols. "Besides," one man told me, rather weakly, " 'Dixie' was wrote by a Yankee anyway." Opponents countered that the symbols represented slavery. They felt they could deprive people of civil rights because, when displayed in public places, the symbols had the chilling effect of inhibiting the expression of real feelings. The symbols taunted blacks and were a divisive force in race relations.

After the official tour of the Dexter Avenue Baptist Church was over, I talked for awhile with the young woman who had shown me through. Gradually she dropped the formal tone she had been using and became more forthcoming. When I asked her about the decision to remove the flag from the state capitol, she said, "Personally, I'm glad the thing isn't up there anymore."

Alexandria, Virginia, a city near where I live, has taken an interesting position on public display of the Confederate flag. This was the boyhood hometown of Robert E. Lee, lying across the Potomac River from Washington, D.C., which has had a majority black population for many years. In a compromise reached in 1970, the flag was removed from public buildings and was flown on only two days—January 19, Lee's birthday, and May 24, Confederate Memorial Day. The city adopted, as part of the compromise, a policy of not asking African-American employees to raise or lower the flag. For over two decades, the city's position had been workable and still, though it was born in the intensity of the civil rights movement, seemed imminently fair.

Few persons I spoke to in the South in the summer of 1993 were interested in compromise, however. Feelings seemed to grow more heated as the southern summer descended full force upon me during the trip.

As I pulled into Mobile, the odometer turned over the ten thousandth mile I had driven since the trip began. Fewer than five minutes later, the left rear tire blew and I lurched and flapped to a stop on a busy highway. While there is no really desirable place for a blowout, the flat tire gods must have been planning this one for weeks. I was on a railroad overpass, with no shoulder. Construction had narrowed the lanes from three to two immediately in front of me, and just to my rear was an entrance ramp. Continuing, even at the risk of damaging the wheel, was impossible because the road narrowed just ahead to two crowded lanes edged with concrete Jersey walls on each side. My only choice was to change the tire where I was.

I turned on the flashers and began emptying my living quarters onto the highway to get at the spare tire. When I began working on the wheel nuts, the danger of the situation became apparent. Cars would hurtle up the on ramp, see me, careen crazily into the adjacent lane of traffic, nearly be hit by cars driving at speed down that lane, swerve back to avoid them and miss me by inches. I ducked a few times, then gave up and stopped looking, trusting to the reflexes and luck of the drivers behind me. I'm not sure how quickly I changed that tire, but I know that it was a new personal record.

I found a store that sold new tires near the waterfront and ordered two to replace the one that had blown out and its partner on the rear, which was also showing signs of wear. While the tires were being installed, I had lunch and a stiff drink to calm my nerves. Mobile is Alabama's only port. It is located on the west side of the dredged Mobile River, not far from where the river empties into the

Named after owner Rick Woodward, Rickwood Field (Birmingham, AL) hosted baseball for the first time in 1911.

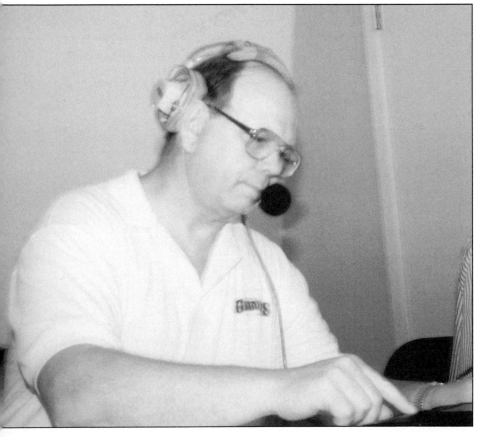

Big Dave Nitz, play-by-play announcer for the Shreveport Captains.

Spar Stadium, Shreveport, LA, "like a huge rotting insect whose tissue had eroded, leaving only the membrane."

Shotgun houses in Mississippi.

Ray Winder Field, Little Rock, AR, before Wilbur Mills Parkway was built just outside the right field fence.
(Courtesy of
Bill Valentine, Arkansas
Travelers Baseball Club)

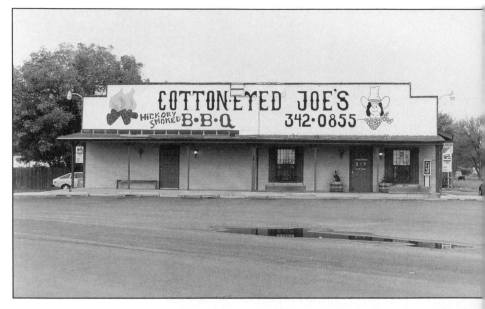

Cotton-Eyed Joe's. From the front porch you can see Route 66, hear the train whistles blow, and smell the hickory burning. (Courtesy of Michael D. Green, Potomac, MD)

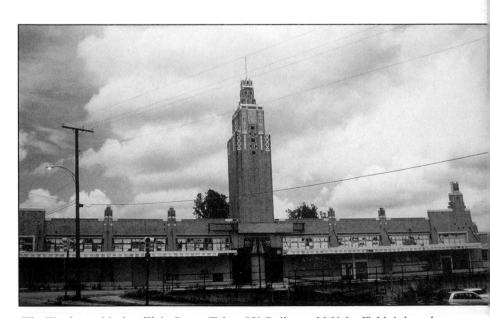

The Warehouse Market, Elgin Street, Tulsa, OK. Built over McNulty Field, it has class even in disrepair.

Lawrence Dumont Stadium, Wichita, KS.

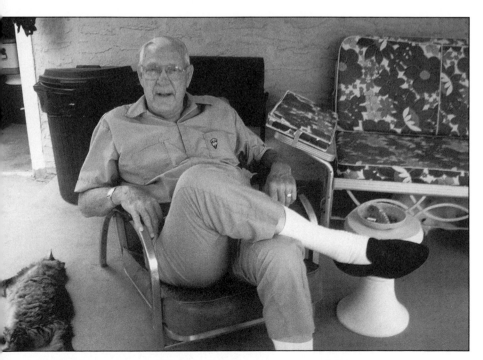

Joe Bauman, at home in Roswell, NM.

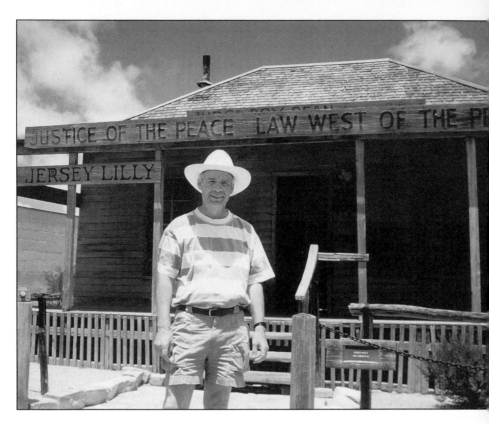

The author, taking a well-deserved break from the toil of attending baseball games.

11

In Evangeline Country

IF I HAD TO PICK A SINGLE baseball situation to epitomize minor league baseball in the south, it would be the Evangeline League. Except for Natchez, Mississippi, and two Texas border towns, the teams were all Louisiana based and within a one-day drive of each other. From 1934 to 1948 (excluding the war years), it ran as a class D league, and moved up to class C in 1949. Its demise came in 1957.

At Nicholls State University in Thibodaux, Louisiana, a history professor has organized a permanent display dedicated to the memory of a vanished minor league. Paul Leslie is codirector of the Evangeline Baseball History Project at Nicholls. Teaching and research are his livelihood. His full-time work is baseball *aficionado*.

Nicholls State is an unlikely looking place for a baseball museum, or any other kind of museum. It is almost treeless and except for the heat layered across the campus, the southern Louisiana flatlands might be the northern tundra. I met Paul Leslie inside the library and we spent a couple of hours looking at the exhibits he had arranged and talking about the Evangeline League.

The 'Vangy was always a fast league for its classification and had remarkable players and teams. In 1948, Ray Sanner of the Houma Indians turned in what was perhaps the most exceptional one-season performance in minor league baseball history. He topped the Evangeline League batting statistics in average, doubles, homeruns, RBIs, and total bases.

Impressive, you say, but not singular? Sanner also won twentyduction manager coordinated their efforts while he explained to me what was happening.

"We use numbers to designate the different cameras instead of locations like third base ground, high home, center field. The usual configuration is five cameras and the numbers were assigned as they were added historically."

The technicians were college interns majoring in television production. Somehow, everyone seemed to be able to talk, laugh, engage in horseplay and yet accomplish what seemed to me to be an overwhelming job of coordination. Each camera had responsibilities. One followed the ball, one shot the pitcher, one picked up the defensive play. A home run, when watched on television, seemed to be a simple unified activity. Yet the sequence was produced by a formula in which the producer cut from one camera following the ball over the fence, to another catching a reaction shot of the pitcher, to another showing the runner rounding second, and so forth. Watching the monitor that contained the images being broadcast, I could see how the sequence was always similar on television, and how much of the real scene was missing.

Television production wasn't only technical. The producer had to know enough baseball, for example, to understand that a manager's second trip to the mound meant a new pitcher, or which pitching counts are favorable for steals so that a camera could be directed to the bullpen or to the basepath, as necessary. A few feet over our heads, oblivious fans crunched peanuts, spilled beer, and yelled the usual epithets at the umpires.

The Captains' fascination with technology also showed on the outfield fence. Pitching speeds, picked up on a radar gun behind home plate, were flashed below a sign "SPEED ON OVER—RED RIVER CHEVROLET" for all the fans to see. The experience was educational. Fastballs came in at speeds in the high eighties, curves in the midseventies, and change-ups as low as fifty-four miles per hour. Fans could appreciate, perhaps for the first time, that batters must contend with speeds varying up to thirty-five miles per hour, in addition to constant changes in location and movement. The star hitter's failure to succeed seven out of ten times was more understandable when one saw the Red River speed board.

On my last day in Shreveport, I set out looking for old Spar Stadium, home of the Captains until 1986. Following a map was impossible: construction on an interstate through the city had made even a recent map useless. Neighborhoods had been bisected and streets simply stopped at the edges of the dirt and concrete. I finally pulled into a used car lot to ask for help.

"You want to sell that pickup?" a salesman asked. "I been looking for a '72 Chevy."

"No, I'm looking for Spar Stadium, the Captains' old ball park. I can't get there following the map."

The salesman helped me plot a way around the highway construction. The park was within half a mile of where we sat, but I was forced to take a four-mile detour. A second salesman, overhearing our conservation, said "That's in the Allendale section. Do you have to go there?" as a third salesman, standing nearby, shook his head gravely. Old ballparks always seem to be in "bad" neighborhoods, according to local people who live in the suburbs. This wasn't the first time I had been implicitly warned against going into a high-crime, poorer, usually all-black district just to see a ballpark.

"I want to take some pictures of it," I said, "before they tear it down."

All three salesman shook their heads in unison.

"I sure wish you'd sell me that truck," one said as I left.

"I can't," I said. "It has to get me to El Paso."

I looked back and saw them all talking together as I walked back to Sweetspot, probably taking bets on whether I would ever make it out of Allendale alive.

Spar had been abandoned because of general deterioration, lack of parking, and the unsavory reputation of the neighborhood surrounding it.

"Fans wouldn't come," Dave Nitz had told me in the press box the night before. "They didn't feel safe."

"Neither did the press," said a writer. The writer's car had been broken into during a game. Others I talked with said that despite the general perception that Spar was unsafe, neither crime nor vandalism had really been a serious problem. Taylor Moore told me that a new highway had been the real problem, as construction severed major arteries to the stadium and driving there became inconvenient. To his, and other club officials' credit, they seemed to take no pleasure in having abandoned the old park. It had just become inevitable for a combination of reasons.

The used car salesman sent me along Texas Street to Spar, and not far from the park, I drove through an inner-city ghost town. A three-block-long strip of shops and businesses had ceased to exist; every single store on both sides of the street was deserted. Freeway construction wasn't to blame here; the small stores had just ceased to be viable. Most weren't even boarded up, just empty.

Spar sat there in the hot sun looking like a huge rotting insect whose membrane had disintegrated, leaving only the skeletal rods. The roof had blown off the grandstand cover and had never been replaced, although the Captains kept using the exceedingly odd-looking field afterwards. I shot a picture through a gaping hole in the left-field wall and then walked through the opening. The base paths were all grass now. The city still mowed the field but the grass was heavily laced with clover. The rest of the park, like Texas Street, had just been left to weather and erode. Faded signs on the outfield walls were barely legible. Seats were cracked and paint was peeling everywhere.

The old park had seen some action. In 1956, right fielder Ken Guettler hit sixty-two home runs for the Shreveport Sports, a Texas League record that still stands. The right-handed batter hit thirty-nine of them through the muggy Louisiana air over the twenty-foot-high left-field wall through which I had just walked. He wore eyeglasses with thick, coke bottle lenses but at 5'11" and 190 pounds had a compact, powerful build. Guettler played in only 140 games in 1956, and that was his last good year. He struggled along for three more years, playing for five different teams but never hitting more than five home runs or batting higher than .232. Guettler retired at age thirty-two, never having registered one major league at bat, and died at age fifty.

One of the most famous denizens of Spar was not a ballplayer, but its longtime groundskeeper, Al Gaedke. When the new park opened in the 1930s, Gaedke moved into a small house in the far right-field corner where he lived alone year round. During the off season, he made the outfield into a small golf course. The owners put a flock of sheep in the park in the 1938–39 winter to keep the grass trimmed, but the experiment ended badly. Dogs got into the ball park and wiped out the sheep, proving, I guess, that humans make more practical groundskeepers than sheep. During Al's tenure, the park was known unofficially as "Gaedke's Gardens."

No one bothered me as I roamed around the old park. In fact, the seats, concession stands, and dugouts disclosed few signs of vandalism, just general decay. Perhaps the wear of time had eroded things to the point where vandalism was superfluous. The old gathering place wasn't going gently, however. Even now, as I looked her over from every angle, there was no doubt that this was a site where people had come to celebrate baseball.

By noon it was already over ninety degrees and I was on my third Dr. Pepper. The hot breeze of the last two days had died; now it was just hot without a breeze. I had been in the South for two months, and had experienced ninety-degree-plus days in Florida but nothing like the bone-wilting, juice-sucking, head-pounding heat of Shreveport.

Not far from Fair Grounds Park, I found some shade under a large oak tree at the edge of a church parking lot and got out a lawn chair. It was too hot to do anything but sit and wait for time to go to the new ballpark with its air-conditioned press box and icy drinks. The church marquee read

ASSEMBLY OF GOD

2000 YEARS UNDER
THE SAME MANAGEMENT

About fifteen feet up in the oak tree a mockingbird sat nervously on her nest, very suspicious of my motives.

Shreveport (198,526) had drawn 207,925 fans through the turn-stiles the previous season. Yet Jackson, last in the Texas League in attendance for 1992, attracted only 140,040 that year, the worst of all the southern AA teams except for Knoxville, with its hopeless 90,387. Jackson's attendance was actually up over 1991, when the club hosted only 114,660 fans, but as of June 6, 1993, the Generals were dead last in Texas League attendance with an average of 2,536 fans per game.

Jackson had never been exactly a bubbling cauldron of baseball activity. Before joining the Texas League in 1975, the city hadn't had a professional baseball team since 1953, when it had an entry in the Cotton States League. In fact, Jackson had been without professional baseball for thirty-eight seasons during the twentieth century, an unusually high figure for a town of its size. A good team playing in a fine park with an excellent location hadn't been able to overcome the lack of a baseball tradition in Jackson, demonstrating that the former ingredients are not the only ones necessary for a successful franchise.

My second night in Jackson I saw one of the most dominating pitching performances of the trip. Alvin Morman, a hard-throwing strikeout pitcher, went six innings with eleven strikeouts, one base on balls, and one unearned run. His fastball was consistently in the low 90s with movement and his hard curve came in at almost slider speed, but with more break. After Morman was removed, I walked down to the bullpen to talk about his performance with some of the other pitchers on the bench. One said that Morman had been taken out because he had thrown a lot of pitches, it was a hot night, and Jackson had pretty well won the first half of the season. I asked if Morman had known that he was in reach of a Texas League record for strikeouts in a single game. (Actually, the Texas League media guide doesn't list the single-game strikeout record for a single pitcher. The team record is twenty-one, and at Morman's six-inning pace, he could have expected only fifteen, as the bottom of the ninth would be unnecessary.)

"Sal [Sal Butera, the manager] says, 'What's the big deal about a AA record, when he's going to the majors?' He may have a major league record ahead of him," said one of the relief pitchers.

The handling of pitchers has been one of the most controversial areas in player development in recent years. Even with careers extended by superior conditioning techniques, modern pitchers can never hope to approach such feats as Cy Young's 511 victories. In the dead ball era, when Cy pitched, pitchers could ease off and lob the ball in, knowing that it wasn't going far. A complete game before 1920 saw, on average, forty fewer pitches than a complete game today. And today, the relentless radar gun exerts pressure to make each throw light up a high number. How much work is enough for a developing pitcher, and how much is too much, is one of the crucial decisions a minor league manager makes.

I saw Morman make one more impressive start, in Arkansas against the Travelers, and then an injury shortened his season. Despite a final 7–1 record and a 2.64 ERA, he didn't pitch the 109 innings required to be listed among *Baseball America's* league leaders at season's end. However, of the eleven pitchers who threw for the Generals in 1993, no one pitched 109 innings, and only one pitcher exceeded one hundred. Jackson ended up with the second highest win total in the Texas League in 1993 with 73 (in a 134-game schedule), but no pitcher recorded even 10 wins for the Generals. The student of minor league baseball who has been grounded in major league reasoning and conditions must constantly adjust his or her expectations.

My four-day stay in Jackson was the most restful period of the trip. The city of Jackson was originally known as LeFleur's Bluff, after a French-Canadian fur trader who founded a trading post on the Pearl River shortly before the arrival of the nineteenth century. LeFleur's Bluff State Park, across the street from Smith-Wills Stadium, now honors this founder. The park's quarter-acre campsites are shaded by huge oak trees and back up to Mayes Lake. Every morning I got up early, walked ten yards to the lake, and caught pan-sized bream on a popping bug with my fly rod. Nothing else worked. I tried a variety of lures and plugs, dry flies, streamers, and spinners and never got a strike, but the bream were absolute fools for the popping bug. I sat in the shade, read, wrote a little, and rested up for the long, hot drives to come in Oklahoma and

CHAPTER TWELVE

After telling him I knew the meaning of the word premises, I took a couple of beers out of the cooler. William seemed to be a good customer at the liquor store, using it as a combination message center and bank as well as for its intended purpose. "Right," he said, taking the beer. "I forgot I was talking to a goddam perfesser."

While we were waiting, he showed me his fishing tackle. He had a large box the size of a suitcase, with twenty or more smaller boxes inside. Each, he explained, was outfitted for a different kind of fishing and was a complete setup in itself. The best fishermen I had fished with, my regular fishing partner Doyle, and Grover, my stepfather, were meticulous about their gear, but I had never seen anything like William's organizational system for comprehensiveness and neatness. It was all the more remarkable because his pickup looked like a rolling junkyard and his house had been chaotic.

I took out my small traveling supply of lures and showed them to him.

"You've caught fish with them goddam thangs?" he wanted to know.

About midafternoon Ink showed up with Henry, a black man somewhere around William's age. They were both covered in grease and hadn't been able to get Henry's truck running. Their arrival naturally called for beers all around to talk things over. As we talked, it became clear that both Ink and William had other black friends, and they seemed to be entirely without prejudice or any hint of a patronizing attitude. I wasn't surprised that this was true of Ink, who seemed to like everyone, but I hadn't expected William to be so open-minded.

While we lounged in the shade, I asked Ink about his name. Was it a nickname?

William laughed loudly when he heard the question. "Tell him your goddam name, Ink!" Without waiting for Ink, he shouted "IN-KILL-LEES!" He repeated the name three times, laughing so hard that he was doubled over, clutching his stomach with one hand and balancing his beer with the other. Ink looked embarrassed. I couldn't understand what William found so hilarious

178

about the name Inkeles, while the shortened version Ink didn't even provoke a smile from him. After he regained some control, he tried to say the name again but just the thought of repeating it caused him to laugh uproariously. Afterwards, I realized that in the day I had spent with him, this was the only time I saw William laugh, or even smile.

We invited Henry on the fishing expedition but he had to get some parts for his stalled pickup. When he left, William and Ink began discussing the purchase of liquor supplies for the fishing trip.

"I have plenty of beer," I offered.

"How much you got?" Ink asked.

"A couple of six packs in the cooler."

They looked at each other in amazement and, without saying a word, turned and walked into the liquor store. They came back in a few minutes with a case of beer and a large sack containing a fifth of bourbon, a pint of vodka, a large bag of Doritos, and an assortment of mixes. Another brief consultation followed, and they went back into the liquor store. I followed them in, unable to imagine what else they could buy. They walked around, pointing at the shelves and discussing various options, finally buying a bottle of brandy and another case of beer. Feeling a little left out, I bought a bottle of white wine to have with the fish at dinner.

"How long are you guys planning to stay at the lake?" I asked as we loaded the liquor.

"We're fixing to stay a couple of days," said Ink.

By the time we left it was late in the afternoon. I had long since forgotten about leaving for Little Rock that day and just hoped we would get to the lost lake before dark. William rode with me again, and Ink led the way in William's truck. On the way, William began to worry about the possibility of my revealing the location of the lake.

"Don't be putting where this goddam place is at in no goddam book," he warned me.

I said I wouldn't.

"You're lucky to be going because the onliest ones that knows about it is me and Ink and Henry and (he named about six other persons)."

179

"I'm not going to tell anyone where it is. You want to blindfold me and drive in yourself?"

He gave the possibility some thought.

"Come on," I said. "I won't tell anyone how to get there."

"Ah hell, you couldn't find the goddam place again anyway."

This sounded more like a comment on my navigational ability than on the remoteness of the lake, but I let it pass. We went from a main highway to a side road, then a gravel road, eventually turning onto a dirt track running through some piney woods, finally emerging into a field overgrown with head-high patches of blackberries and other brambles, where we drove alongside a small creek lined with trees and came to an earthen dam.

The "lake" was disappointingly small, covering less than a couple of acres, and the banks were so choked with undergrowth that access was limited to only a few spots. Reeds growing several yards out into the water promised to make fishing even more difficult. William peeled out of the pickup and by the time I had opened the back of Sweetspot, he was established at the most open fishing spot and had already hooked a medium-sized bass. He caught another one as I was assembling my telescoping rod, and another as Ink and I walked over to the pond. After landing each fish, William threw it about ten feet up on the bank and cast again.

"William's a good fisherman," said Ink, needlessly.

"Why is he throwing the fish up here?" I asked Ink.

"Waiting for me to string 'em."

"Aren't you going to fish?" I asked him.

"Some," he said.

I looked at him. "I guess you and William are pretty good friends."

"William's a good guy, really. He's bad to drink, though." Ink was carrying a beer and pulling at it between sentences.

I walked around the small pond and began casting toward one end. The fish were there, and they were easy to catch, though none of us hooked any of the behemoths that William insisted were plentiful. I watched William while he fished. He hadn't seemed particularly athletic in movement or even graceful in general, but with a fishing rod in his hand, he was transformed. Watching him play a two-pound largemouth bass was like listening to the rhythm of a piece of classical music. Once I heard him tell Ink that there was a large bass behind a stump, and when Ink cast he said: "Not *that* goddam stump." With that, his arm tensed and he unleashed the longest cast I have ever seen, sailing over the dark distant mark, then flicking his wrist to make the topwater lure change directions and angle around the surface obstacle. A fish struck, William set the hook, and when the bass broke the water it was seen to be the biggest catch of the day.

This "lost lake" must have been a former farm pond, probably stocked with bass and bream at one time, and now lying unused because the farm had gone under. We had passed an old barn on the way in, and I had seen other ruins at the end of the overgrown field. The pond was undoubtedly on private property, and we were obviously trespassing. I began to suspect that some of the day's procrastination was deliberately timed to get us here late in the day to minimize the chance of discovery.

In less than an hour we stopped fishing and sorted through the catch, keeping a few for dinner and releasing the others. I fileted four bass weighing between one and two pounds, and took out my camping utensils. My one-burner stove would have taken too long to cook the fish, so William rigged up a grill from part of a bed frame he had in the back of the pickup, overlaying it with pieces of corrugated metal used in reinforcement of concrete. In the confusion of getting the trip underway, none of us had thought about dishes to accompany the fish. I produced a few pieces of fruit from the cooler, and offered William and Ink each a container of yogurt. They both looked at the yogurt tubs suspiciously and refused to even consider them.

After a dinner of crisply fried fish, Doritos, and peaches, the mosquitoes came in earnest and I climbed into the back of Sweetspot to go to sleep. William and Ink, apparently impervious to the insect attacks, stayed up by the fire, drinking and talking. At one point, I heard Ink say, "Ernie's a pretty good guy, isn't he? I mean for a perfesser and everything?"

"I guess," said William, "but he worries about every goddam thang. He'll be a nervous wreck time he gets to El Paso."

181

The next morning I took US 49 out of Jackson for a leisurely drive north through the Mississippi Delta country. The Delta region was bounded on the west by the Mississippi River and on the east by the hills of central Mississippi. The soil, planted in cotton and soybeans, was fertile, the land was flat, and the air was sultry. At Yazoo City, I took 49 west through the heart of the Delta. Yazoo City was a member of the short-lived Delta League of 1904, a class D six-team minor league. Only two of the teams, Clarksdale and Yazoo City, were in the Delta region, but the shaky little league folded after only one season anyway, before anyone could demand a more appropriate name.

I pulled off the road just north of where state road 14 comes into US 49W to watch a crop dusting plane at work. The small yellow biplane flew close to the ground, releasing spray over the crops and giving a section of highway 14 a dose of the insecticide before banking sharply and going back for another run.

The little town of Midnight, Mississippi, sat north of the fields being sprayed, about twenty buildings hunched together against the late morning sun. The town was surrounded on all four sides by crops, planted in straight lines across the flat terrain. At the one-room post office, a woman was swatting flies, squashing them against the front window that looked out on the street. She told me that this office was the only "Midnight" listed in the U.S. Postal Service *Zip Code Directory*. The name, she said, derived from a poker game played many years ago among several wealthy plantation owners on the Delta. It was a high stakes game and one player lost a large parcel of land. The winner, noting the time when he won the hand, announced to the others that he would call his new acquisition "Midnight," and when a small town was later established, it bore the same name. I wrote out a postcard to some friends in Maryland and gave it to the woman. She postmarked the card with the town name and went back to her fly swatter.

The Mississippi Delta country came closest to any place I had been to the South of my imagination. Rows of green crops stretched across the flat, rich soil; weathered shotgun shacks lined the hot, sleepy little streets; and people moved slowly in the steamy heat. Narrow, muddy rivers seemed barely to flow. White farmers in rough pickup trucks raised an index finger slowly in greeting, and black people averted their eyes. US 49W was a concrete ribbon through the land of cotton, the heart of Dixie's land.

At Indianola I took a small country road marked SR 448 over to US 61, and turned directly north. A sun devil kicked up in an unplanted field to my left, and I drove along wishing I had someone along to share the South with me.

I took US 61 north through Clarksdale and looked at the map. Memphis was only forty miles or so to the north. I thought about spending the night there, even though the Chicks weren't in town, to see what Phil Stukenborg was writing and see if anyone else I knew was around. Then I envisioned trying to explain to Eric McCool how I had left three weeks earlier to work my way west, and was now back in the same place. I turned into the sun on US 49 and crossed the big river into Arkansas at Helena, my third crossing of the trip.

Walking through the turnstiles at Ray Winder Field in Little Rock, Arkansas, tripped a magic wire somewhere, and I was back in the 1940s. Alfreda Wilson, the longtime Arkansas Travelers' organist, was pounding out a patriotic tune, and all the concession stands were human scale and humanely priced. By the time I had walked down to a seat behind home plate, I was trying to think of a way to convince Zena to move to Little Rock.

From the first row of seats behind home plate, I could see the right fielder only from the knees up, and the center fielder's feet were missing. The field had a pronounced hump, with the infield forming the apex. The right field situation was in fact a considerable improvement this year; formerly, the right fielder wasn't visible at all from the third base dugout. Visiting managers had to walk almost to the foul line to position their right fielders. Just off both base paths and behind home plate, a noticeable slope, dropping a couple of feet, provided an interesting sensation for fielders chasing foul balls. Runners taking a wide turn around third had to puff back up hill to get home. The broadleaf grass had a liberal sprinkling of clover, which was blooming brightly in June, making the field resemble a close-cut version of a suburban lawn.

In the first inning, a batter on the visiting Jackson Generals team

183

hit a pop foul behind home plate and it drifted back toward the screen. The catcher took it inches from the screen, and just a few feet from where I was sitting.

"Nice catch," I said.

"Thanks," he replied. I mentally chalked up another tally mark favoring minor league baseball over the distant action in the big leagues.

During the game I walked around to see the field from different angles. Beer flowed freely in the left field stands, home of the "Hooters Trav Rooters," who ranked with the rowdiest in baseball. On the third base side, ground level fans were literally on the field. Seats had been built out into foul territory past the third base dugout. This may be the only park in baseball where some fans had a closer view of the action than managers and players. Children could lean into the end of the dugout and bother the players full time during the game.

I reached the pressbox, suspended from the grandstand roof, by a catwalk. Inside the cramped quarters, revolving ceiling fans tried to cool the corps of writers and club officials, pressed together in the tiny space. Late in the game, an invasion of moths, flying around by the thousands, descended on the playing field and added to the general din that was Ray Winder Field on a warm summer night.

The park, opened in 1932, was of steel and concrete construction with a roof canopy over the grandstand. Left field was 325 feet, center 405 feet, and right field, a short 300 feet away. Wilbur Mills Freeway now runs immediately outside right field, so a 55-foot right-field screen has been erected to protect motorists. A home run launched over the screen usually clears the parkway as well.

Ray Winder is one of the few sports stadiums owned by its baseball club. The Arkansas Travelers, in turn, are owned, technically, by fans, 1,200 stockholders who hold varied amounts of interest in the club. Realistically, the Travelers belong to Bill Valentine, their general manager since 1976 and one of the longest tenured general managers in minor league baseball.

Bill is a former major league umpire who, together with Al Salerno, formed an umpire's union in 1968. They were fired, ostensibly for incompetence, and never umpired again. Bill wasn't incompetent, but unionizing was a few years ahead of its time. He returned to his home town of Little Rock and did radio and then television reporting and announcing for two years. A stint as assistant director, and then director, of the Arkansas Republican party followed. In December of 1975, Valentine was offered the job of general manager of the Arkansas Travelers. He saw the neglected condition of the ballpark, went over the low attendance figures and generally unpromising picture of the club's account books, and told them flatly: "You can't afford me." They met his terms, though, and the alliance was formed.

In 1975, the year before Bill Valentine took over, the season's attendance was 64,000. In his first year as general manager, the total jumped to over 90,000. By 1978, that figure had doubled to 184,000, and in five of the past seven years, Arkansas, with the second smallest market of any Texas League city, has led the league in attendance. Recently, only Tulsa, with its larger, more modern stadium and bigger population base, had consistently outdrawn the Travelers.

I met Bill on a hot June afternoon in the business office at Ray Winder. Usually Bill didn't arrive at the ballpark until after noon, but on game days this still meant that he put in an eleven-hour day. The meager club office housed one of the smallest staffs in double A baseball, smaller in fact than many at the class A level.

"We have to operate differently from clubs who have rich owners," Bill explained. "The Travelers don't fly anywhere. Anywhere we go, we go by bus."

The general rule in the Texas League is that most clubs go by bus to games with clubs in their division, and fly to cities in the other division. "We have a sleeper bus with a VCR and a refrigerator, and we're centrally located. We don't fly anywhere," Bill told me. "We don't fly anywhere."

Bill repeated sentences in a sharp, staccato delivery whenever he wanted to emphasize his point.

"Come with me," he said. "You have to walk your property. You have to walk your property."

We were off on an inspection tour that lasted for two hours. In

185

appearance, Valentine fit exactly the general image of a baseball umpire. Broad and compact, with a crew-cut, he had a stern and usually unsmiling face, and a firm, definite manner. His demeanor was suggestive of a drill sergeant in the army. He noticed the most minute details as we walked around the park, such as a clock hanging crookedly, and barked orders to the next employee he saw to get it fixed.

We walked out to the stands. "Look down that aisle," Bill directed. "What do you see? What do you see?"

"Nothing. Nothing." I was getting into the rhythm of the conversation.

"No gum, no stickiness from cokes, no trash. This is every day. Every game. The whole park is the same way. Let's go into the johns."

We walked into an immaculately clean rest room. "The most important reason women won't come to the ballpark is dirty rest rooms. See that?" He gestured to a container fastened to the wall. "Hand lotion. What other ballpark has hand lotion? You ever see another woman's rest room in a ball park with hand lotion?"

I admitted that I hadn't, then added that I had never been in another woman's rest room, period.

The men's room was equally clean. "See this," he said, pointing to an elevated area in front of a urinal. It had the appearance of a ceramic tile pitcher's mound. "For boys. They're too short to reach big urinals." He stood on the mound with his back to me as he delivered the explanation. Thinking he was just demonstrating the mound, I walked around to look, then saw that he was using the facility, never missing a beat in the running commentary.

Next we inspected the concession stands, tucked traditionally under the grandstand. The taco stand had $18,000 worth of stainless steel formed into shelves Bill had designed to expedite taco service. I was impressed. Five hours before game time and the park was spotless. None of the newer parks I had seen could match it; most of the older ones were ill kept by comparison.

Back in the club offices, I talked to Bill about the franchise's success. When he arrived in 1976, minor league clubs were being sold for almost nothing; sometimes all a buyer had to do was to take over the debts. The Travelers' amazing increase in attendance ran counter to the period's general decline in baseball attendance. How did he do it?

"Promotions," Bill said. "I started a midget on opening day 1976. Sent out the word I was looking for one and one day in late winter, sitting where I am now, the door opens and I don't see anybody." (A four-foot counter ran at a right angle from the club office's door.) "Then Roscoe Steadman comes around the corner and says, 'I hear you're looking for a little person. I'm your man.' He was three inches shorter than Bill Veeck's midget. That's how tall he was."

Unlike the 3'7", sixty-five-pound Eddie Gaedel whom Veeck put in to pinch hit for the St. Louis Browns in 1951, Roscoe didn't take four balls and trot down to first. He grounded out, then was "ejected" for arguing the call at first. A woman, about Roscoe's height and posing as his wife, ran onto the field and hit the umpire with her purse. The fans loved it, and the promotions frenzy was on.

By promotions, Bill didn't mean on-field contests between innings. There were none of those. Promotions really meant giving away tickets. Businesses would sponsor a night, paying the club a fee and issuing free tickets to get customers to come to their establishments and pick them up.

"I can make more money by letting people in free than I can by charging," Bill said.

"How can you make money doing that?" I asked.

"Concessions! Concessions!" From a desk drawer, Bill pulled records that showed, he said, that you could make more money by giving away tickets than by charging for them. "The bottom line is how much money you make, not how many people pay for a ticket. You promote your product, and when people come they'll buy your concessions."

Bill told me that he had coined the slogan, "The Greatest Show on Dirt" to use in the Travelers' promotional literature. "The circus people heard about it and sent word that they'd sue us if we didn't quit using it. I changed the programs and pamphlets to 'The Greatest Game on Dirt' and that satisfied them."

that they're in the Texas League; that's like the league they're in?" (Fan #4 was a teenager.)

Fan #5: "I think it's in the newspaper. I haven't checked it for years, but that's where you can find out if you want to know, in the newspaper."

I concluded my survey at that point. Four of five, or 80 percent of my small sample, did not know where the Travelers were in the standings. The old umpire had made the right call again.

13

Return to T-Town

ALMOST IMMEDIATELY AFTER I crossed the state line between Arkansas and Oklahoma, a car whizzed around the pickup and three young men inside extended their arms outside the car windows with "thumbs up" signs, good natured smiles on their faces. Sweetspot had personalized license plates that read, "SOONERS." The plates were a double tribute to the pickup's state of residence for its first seventeen years and to the mighty University of Oklahoma football team. I drove along, basking in my new-found popularity, troubled only a little by thinking about the reception the plates would get later in Texas.

I had left Arkansas on a small highway to pick up what was left of old Route 66. The "Mother Road," as John Steinbeck dubbed it in *The Grapes of Wrath,* ran 2,448 twisting, snaky miles from Chicago to Los Angeles in its heyday. First authorized in 1926, it was finished by the midthirties. From Joplin, Missouri, the route jogged straight west and made a half loop through only thirteen miles of Kansas before dipping down into Oklahoma. In 1984, the fabled byway was declassified. Today it either lies under interstates, bears different road numbers, or sits unused with grass sprouting up through the old road bed. In little more than half a century, the highway was born, became a main thoroughfare, lapsed into obsolescence, and finally became a nostalgia piece. In the past few years, historic preservation societies have sprung up along the old road; and the familiar US 66 markers have reappeared to guide the curious through the small and large towns it once enlivened.

I hooked up with the old highway in the little town of Commerce, Oklahoma, and stopped for awhile to visit the former haunts of the Commerce Comet. The northeast quadrant of Oklahoma has given birth to a surprising number of remarkable people—Will Rogers, Jim Thorpe, Woody Guthrie—but Mickey Mantle has been the only Oklahoman from this area to hit a baseball 565 feet. At the police station where I asked for directions, the officer on duty told me a few Mantle stories and sent me to the last place Mickey had lived in Commerce before moving to Dallas. The red brick bungalow on Maple Street, just a couple of blocks off Route 66, was small but well kept and had a swimming pool in the yard. Mickey had lived in several houses in Commerce and in other little towns in northeastern Oklahoma, most of them meager, battered places weathered to the same color as the piles of gray chat they were tucked among. Mounds of chat, the dead-looking residue from the lead and zinc mines that ran underground everywhere in this corner of the state, still swell out of the prairie around Commerce today, now sprouting green undergrowth.

Mickey was taught the art of switch-hitting by his father, Mutt Mantle, who had been a semipro ballplayer in the tristate area of Oklahoma, Kansas, and Missouri. Mutt worked by day in the dangerous zinc mines of the Eagle-Picher company, whose underground caverns stretched all the way to Joplin, twenty miles away in Missouri. Under his father's guidance, Mickey developed into a high school three-sport legend in northeastern Oklahoma. When Yankee scout Tom Greenwade signed him in 1949, he was assigned to Independence, Kansas, in the class D Kansas-Oklahoma-Missouri (K-O-M) League. Ancient buses carried his team along Route 66 and smaller two-lane blacktops to Bartlesville, Carthage, Chanute, Pittsburg, and Miami, and to a league championship. Mickey hit .313 in eighty-nine games but as a shortstop recorded forty-seven errors. The following season he moved up to class C ball with the Jopin Miners in the Western Association. In towns like Topeka, Kansas, and Muskogee, Oklahoma, Mantle blistered the ball. He topped the league with a .383 batting average, 141 runs scored, and 199 hits. Although he didn't win the home run title, word began to spread about the distance he was getting when he connected. Also, Yankee officials were beginning to speculate that Mickey might be more comfortable in the outfield. His erratic play at shortstop continued and he made four errors in the All-Star game in Muskogee. At season's end, the eighteen-year-old Mickey was called up by the Yankees, his apprenticeship in the lower minors over.

I saw him once in the early years. In 1953 or early 1954, when I was a high school freshman, he came to a winter basketball game in Claremore to watch his younger twin brothers, Roy and Ray, play in a tournament. He sat quietly, even then staring straight ahead as if disconnected from his surroundings, hesitant to make eye contact lest strangers attempt to strike up a conversation. As I remember, no one approached him. He had played through two solid seasons with the Yankees by then, and the media were forecasting great things for him, but he hadn't yet acquired mythic proportions. Late in his career, when I lived in Washington, D.C., I was always trying to see him play when the Yankees visited the Senators. He had trouble registering four hundred at bats in those seasons, and invariably would be out of the starting lineup for one injury or another when I went to a game. Mickey seemed to lose interest in baseball as his physical skills deteriorated. Sometime in the late 1960s, he put together a five for five game against the Senators. After the game, reporters asked him if he had ever done that before. No, Mantle said, that was his first time going five for five. Someone checked and learned that he actually had done it before, and had forgotten.

Roy and Ray Mantle, four years younger than Mickey, were outstanding high school athletes. The Yankees signed them to contracts and both played a season in the class D Sooner State League, each hitting over .300. They were also fast, and in spring training with the Yankees the following year, they outran everyone except Mickey, who could fly in those days. Oklahoma sports reporters confidently began predicting an all-Mantle Yankee outfield within a few years, but it wasn't to be. Roy suffered a career-ending leg injury while running out a base hit, and Ray lost two years to the army after being drafted. He never went back to baseball.

On the Oklahoma prairie outside Commerce where Mickey used

193

to play, the Sooner Pride Committee has raised a large sign. It proclaims an intent to put up a sixteen-foot monument to the Commerce Comet. A thermometer measured donated funds. One hundred twenty-five thousand dollars are needed for the monument, and the red mercury was only at the $30,000 mark when I saw it. If all the funds have to come from the little town of Commerce, which appears to be anything but prosperous, Mickey's monument might never materialize.

I followed Route 66 where it was still possible, working my way roughly southwest through the small towns down deeper into Oklahoma. In some stretches, the fabled road bisects stretches of vacant prairie, under a huge blue sky full of brilliant white cloud formations stretching from horizon to horizon, and I saw the same scene that Ma Barker and Bonnie and Clyde had sped through sixty years earlier, flying hell-bent away from their latest bank robberies. In Foyil, I drove over the original pale pink Route 66 concrete, which hadn't been resurfaced since it was first laid.

Route 66 runs through one end of Claremore, my birthplace. The town is better known for the Will Rogers Memorial, located on a ridge on the west side. Willie, as he was called in his youth, was actually born on a ranch about twelve miles to the north, near what became the small town of Oologah. "No one but an Indian could pronounce Oologah," said the part Cherokee Rogers, "so I just say I'm from Claremore."

I intended to sleep in a real bed at my mother's house for a week and commute down to watch the Tulsa Drillers play. My first stop in Claremore, though, was the city cemetery. The quiet graveyard sits on a gentle hill sloping down to a cow pasture. In the distance, trucks roll by on the Will Rogers Turnpike. Flowers, many now brown and brittle in the Oklahoma heat, sat uncollected on graves where they'd been laid on Memorial Day, a few weeks earlier. I walked around in the still air, pausing at each family grave to remember something about the resident: an uncle; a cousin who had died within the past year; two sets of grandparents; the same cousin's father; my father; my stepmother; two half brothers who died in infancy before I was born; an aunt and uncle on my father's side; another cousin; and a great-grandmother whom I had never known. Some sort of turning point in a person's life is reached when more members of his or her family lie inside the cemetery than walk around outside.

T-Town was my father's name for Tulsa. I'm not sure how much of its history he knew, but the nickname was a natural. The Locha-pokas, a band of Creeks in Alabama, were uprooted and force-marched along the deadly Trail of Tears in 1836. They brought with them ashes from the sacred fire at their *tulsey*, their old town, and started a new council fire, hoping that a reborn life would rise from the ashes like the phoenix. The oak underneath which the council fire was started still stands at Eighteenth Street and Cheyenne Avenue in Tulsey Town, fenced in and surrounded by the white man's buildings.

Professional baseball in T-Town is played at Fifteenth and Yale, on a corner of the State Fairgrounds, in Driller Stadium. The park opened in 1981 as Sutton Stadium, named after oilman Robert Sutton, who donated most of the funds for its construction. In 1983, when Sutton was allegedly involved in an illegal oil-pricing scheme, the name was quietly changed to Tulsa County Stadium. Tulsa has long been one of the mainstays in the Texas League. For years the team was known as the Oilers, until the more suggestive and macho name Drillers was adopted. A mock oil derrick standing just to the right of center field outside the fence reminded fans of Tulsa's former image as the "Oil Capital of the World." Tulsa long ago ceased to be a dominant oil producer, and when I visited the park, the wooden edifice was under wraps, with an uncertain future.

Driller Stadium's grandstand seating was originally built as three distinct structures, with a smallish, red grandstand behind home plate and two larger stands running down the baselines. Over the years, builders have filled in the space between the stands, replaced the original artificial turf, and added new offices and a stylish press box. Today Driller Stadium hosts what is really a AAA operation with a AA classification. The organization was one of five finalists for a AAA franchise in the early 1990s, and obtaining one seems merely a matter of time.

195

Dimensions of the field have remained unchanged since it was built. Before batting practice, I walked around the outfield walls. The grass was a deep green, perfectly manicured, and kept fresh in the Oklahoma sun with gallons of water and a ryegrass mixture. The infield looked as if no foot had ever scarred its surface. Left field, which butted up against Fifteenth Street, was 335 feet down the line and a short 349 feet to the left field power alley. Home runs fell into the street, but so far drivers had been lucky. Once, I was told, a home run hit the street and bounced into the open window of a car, causing no damage and pleasantly surprising the driver. Dead center was marked at 390 feet, while right field ran 340 feet to the foul pole with a 368-foot power alley, making it a little harder for left-handed batters to spray Yale Avenue with home runs.

The park had the largest seating capacity in the Texas League, with 10,722 seats, and the team consistently drew enough fans to justify its size. Formerly a multiuse stadium, it was now used only for baseball. And it drew real baseball fans. On my first night in the park, I discovered that Tulsa spectators, unlike those in most other minor league parks, still booed home town players as well as visitors when they performed poorly.

A month earlier, a killer tornado had wiped out part of the small town of Catoosa, just east of Tulsa. The previous day's game had been canceled because of more tornado threats. The stands were constructed of frail-looking aluminum; and practically the only things made of concrete were the rest rooms, which sat on the concourse like cinder block, wartime bunkers. Signs at each restroom entrance read "Designated Storm Shelter."

The canceled game had added more misery to Tulsa's scheduling problems. The team was in the midst of a "home stand from hell": thirteen home games in twelve days, a stretch that would now include two doubleheaders, if no more cancellations occurred. I had been running into trouble with Texas League scheduling myself. Trying to plot an itinerary across the southwest was difficult because teams would typically come in for a five- or six-day stay instead of the usual three or four game series. This year's schedule was the brainchild of league president Tom Kayser, who was forever explaining its necessity.

I met Tom on my first evening in Tulsa, where he had stopped on a swing through all the cities in the league. He was a young, energetic man who looked like a recent MBA graduate from a Big East Ivy League school. The contrast between Tom Kayser and Southern League president Jimmy Bragan was like that between a modern computer and a manual Remington. The only similarity I saw, and the only one that really needed to exist, was a commitment to the well-being of baseball. Tom came into the press box before the game and began making suggestions to the newspaper writers for stories about umpires and other ideas he had been thinking about. When he introduced himself, I had an inkling that I should recognize the name. Even his face was familiar, from pictures, I realized later, on all the Texas League publications. "Are you with the Drillers?" I asked, thinking maybe he was one of General Manager Joe Preseren's assistants.

"No, no!" he said with conviction. "I'm the league president!"

One of Tom's projects for 1993 was to reduce average game time. He instructed umpires to have hitters ready when warmup pitches were finished and told coaches to jog to the mound for conferences with pitchers. The latter directive wasn't particularly successful, especially when a relief pitcher needed additional time to warm up, but by year's end, the league game average was two hours, thirty-five minutes, ten minutes less than in 1992. His goal for the following year (1994) was two hours, twenty minutes.

Tom's emphasis on efficiency might seem to run counter to the relaxed tradition of baseball, but things have gone too far in the other direction in recent years. I like to watch baseball played, but waiting while a self-absorbed batter adjusts every reachable piece of uniform between every pitch is merely irritating. Besides, Tom Kayser approached things with a good-natured ebullience. During one game, he joined me behind home plate and pulled out a stopwatch. He didn't really time anything while we sat there, preferring to talk baseball. The umpires and players saw the watch, however, as he intended.

Umpires are the direct responsibility of a minor league president, treat his arthritis with radium water. A picture from that time shows him standing in front of part of the famous gun collection; a solid-looking, silver-haired old Cherokee wearing a western string tie and a rattle-snake belt. Ferguson wrote, "While Tincup's tantalizing slider is gone, his keen memory is still there."

After they tore the Mason down, Ben moved across the street to the Will Rogers Hotel. When he died, his funeral was sung in Cherokee. I asked Frankie if he had been ill.

"I think he just decided to die and did. He willed himself to die. The old Cherokees could do that." Maybe so. Ben Tincup did things that few others have done. And once, in 1917, he achieved a state to which none of us are ever supposed to aspire. He was, according to the rules of baseball, perfect.

Although the Mason was gone and the Will Rogers stood on its last legs, one institution in Claremore was going strong. Cotton-Eyed Joe's Hickory Smoked Bar-b-Que Restaurant was still chopping and smoking and dishing out succulent, tasty pork ribs. My sister, Janice, who has a Ph.D. in ribs, has moved around a lot in her life. When she arrives in a new city, her job is to find the best barbecue place in the area, and then I come to visit. Based on her choices of prime places over the years, I have distilled the essential characteristics of a barbecue joint. The restaurant should be in a converted house, once fashionable but now in a less-desirable section of town, with the pit set up in the back yard so that the effluvium of wood smoke tickles your nostrils as soon as the car door opens. The house should be near a railroad track, so that the sounds of a train whistle and the taste of ribs become unconsciously intertwined over the years, and the tables inside should have plastic covers for a fast swipe with a wet rag as the customers leave. A little garish neon over the door is crucial, and a limited menu is a must. Barbecue places that offer chicken and fish and vegetables du jour just aren't focused enough to concentrate on their main business. Furnishings should date back at least twenty-five years, and if they do, you have some assurance that prices and selections haven't kept pace with the times either.

Cotton-Eyed Joe's has all the imperatives and wonderful ribs besides, with crunchy cole slaw and tangy baked beans. On the other side of the railroad tracks, about forty yards in front of the house-turned-restaurant, runs storied Route 66. I may be biased toward Cotton-Eyed Joe's, for the barbecue joint is part of my family history. In the late 1930s, my Aunt Dell married a young Irishman named Walker Casey. To support three children, Walker worked in the zinc mines of northeast Oklahoma, the same mines near Picher where Mutt Mantle, and later Mickey, worked. One day he tamped dynamite into a hole in the mine wall that already had explosives in it. He was killed instantly, and with part of the insurance money, Aunt Dell bought an old house next to the Frisco railroad tracks in Claremore. Later, she married a carpenter who expanded the cold, draughty house. But the house was never large and it bulged with their ten children, and hangers-on like my sister and me, who spent many mealtimes at the long dining room table, competing for the home grown vegetables and Kool Aid.

When my aunt and uncle moved across town, their daughter and son-in-law converted the old place into a barbecue restaurant. Now the business belongs to one of their offspring. People pour into Cotton-Eyed Joe's and plunk down hard cash for meals today, but the old place saw a lot of mealtimes over the years before the neon sign went up.

My mother and I had lunch at the restaurant one hot midday before I drove down to Tulsa to go to "work." We sat in what had been the living room and talked about family associations. On the wall was a large, shiny Bowie knife, hand made by my Uncle Troy, mounted on a wooden plaque. The ribs came with a dark, rich sauce created by one of my aunts, though which one is in dispute.

I told my mother that, when I was young and spent the night with my cousins, we would sneak out of a back room window and run the half mile downtown to the Yale Theater. When the ticket booth closed after the last show began, we would slip through the lobby and watch the movie already in progress. She took the news silently and looked at me uncertainly, not sure what the appropriate punishment was for a middle-aged man who confesses to a youthful transgression.

"Now you tell me," she said finally.

Barry Lewis, a Tulsa sportswriter, was temporarily filling in as scorekeeper for the Drillers. Watching him keep score one night, I asked if he had seen the new computerized systems. He looked down at his score sheet, with its complicated system of symbols and cross-checks, and said: "When I get through scoring a game, the sheet isn't just rows of numbers. It's a work of art."

One day I skipped batting practice and followed Eleventh Street, the former Highway 66, down toward the center of Tulsa. Where Eleventh Street bent and ascended a slight rise before penetrating the tall buildings of central Tulsa stood a magnificent structure called the Warehouse Market. The old building was an example of a type of art deco architecture called Pueblo Deco, and it was on the hit list. I wanted to see the landmark once again before it disappeared, or was "saved" as the facade of a chain hardware store.

The site is special for another reason. The warehouse was built over McNulty Park, home of the Western Association Class A Tulsa Oilers. McNulty was built in only twenty-two days in February 1919, and was the location of Tulsa professional baseball until 1929. It seated seven thousand but was cozy even by pre-Ruthian dead ball standards. Left field was 310 feet, center was 320 feet, leaving left center essentially without a power alley. Right field, hemmed in by the Midland Valley Railroad tracks, was only 274 feet. I could still see remnants of the rail bed and even some of the old tracks.

In the park's eleven-year existence, Tulsa led the league in hitting seven times. McNulty was also the setting of one of baseball's most curious records. From 1922 through part of the 1925 season, center fielder Lyman Lamb ignited a barrage of doubles unequaled before or after. In 1924, Lamb set the organized record for doubles in one season with an incredible 100. Playing in 168 games that season, he amassed 261 hits and an impressive .373 average. Lamb's nearest rival for doubles in a season was Paul Waner, who hit seventy-five in 1925 but was playing in the 200-game season of the Pacific Coast League. The closest any non-PCL hitter came to Lamb's record was Ervin Beck of Toledo who hit 71 in 1900, a sum equaled by Lamb himself in 1923 when he was warming up for the all-time mark. In three consecutive McNulty years, Lamb reached totals of 68, 71, and 100 doubles.

At Driller Stadium later that evening, I asked Barry Lewis and fellow sportswriter John Ferguson about the doubles record. Between them existed an encyclopedic command of the game's history. Barry speculated that ground rules at McNulty had played a role, but that seemed unlikely. There was no direct record of such rules, at least that I found, and balls over the fence obviously were credited as home runs. Mule Washburn and Yank Davis of the Oilers hit forty-eight and forty-two homers, respectively, and Lamb himself chipped in with nineteen in his record year of 1924. The right-handed hitting Lamb later recalled trying to pull everything he hit over the third baseman's head, so he was trying for doubles. Even harder to understand with McNulty's configuration, however, is how the short fence in left center was conducive to doubles. Anything that stayed in the park would have been a short throw to second. Lamb had some speed, averaging fifteen stolen bases per year in his three full years at McNulty, but he never led even his own team in that department.

In 1925, Lamb was made playing manager of the Tulsa Oilers. When the team faltered, playing in seventh place at midseason, Lamb was fired and played out his career in a number of towns in the Southwest. In three and a half seasons at McNulty, Lamb averaged .349 and about seventy doubles per full season. In every other park, he hit .292. His highest non-McNulty season for doubles was forty-seven, hit for Wichita Falls in the Texas League in 1927. Rarely has a player's hitting stroke and a ballpark's layout meshed so nicely as in those few years on Elgin Avenue in Tulsa.

McNulty Park patrons saw Babe Ruth, who played in a 1929 exhibition game there when the hapless St. Louis Browns, Tulsa's major league affiliate, inexplicably beat the Yankees. Red Grange played in an exhibition there, and Jack Dempsey went a few rounds before the park was razed in 1929 to clear ground for the Warehouse Market. Eight years earlier the ballpark had been part of an unseemly spectacle when life and baseball intersected in an unusual way. Tulsa was the scene of one of the nation's bloodiest general direction of fly balls, the coach would send me in, usually after an especially clumsy error. As I ran toward the outfield, the monster would see me and start in, yelling loudly: "ATTABOY GREEN, YOU'RE THE MAN, GET IN HERE BABE, YOU'RE THE ONE!" When we passed, he would snarl viciously but softly so no one else heard: "You little piss ant! You better miss everything that comes out here! You catch a fly and I'll kick your ass up between your shoulders after the game! You hear me, Green?" Even routine catches had elements of heroism that season.

Baseball is played somewhere else in Collinsville now. The old backstop is gone, the benches are gone, the few rows of bleacher seats are gone, and the basepaths and infield have gone to grass. Little is left to indicate that all the catching, throwing, batting, spitting, glory, embarrassment, and cursing each other ever happened at all.

14

A Southwestern Sultan of Swat

I STAYED IN TULSA FOR A WEEK, longer than at any other stop on the trip, and left there more reluctantly than any other place except my home in Maryland. Tulsa baseball was in good hands, though. General Manager Joe Preseren and his staff had been hospitable, and even the ballpark food had been good. Hot fajitas on the menu indicated that the Southwest was close. I had said my goodbyes, arranged to meet Tom Kayser at a future stop, and begun driving west. The trip was beginning to wind down so I tried to focus on the people and places still on the calendar.

I wasn't quite finished with Oklahoma. Forty miles west of Tulsa, the small town of Yale was one-time home to the great Sac and Fox athlete, Jim Thorpe. His plain, five-room gray clapboard bungalow was open to the public and I stopped to learn more about his life. The little place wasn't inundated with business; I was the first person to sign in two days. A solitary woman served as caretaker and guide.

"Two of Jim's daughters still live in Yale," she told me. The house had been their home as girls and had served Jim as a base of operations. He traveled a lot even after the Olympics and his professional sports careers were over. And like other famous athletes, he didn't handle retirement well. The death of his young son at age three, when Jim was thirty, exacerbated an already serious drinking problem, which continued the rest of his life. As a laborer, movie extra, lecturer, and, during World War II, a merchant marine, he wandered the country as a lost soul.

The little house managed to convey a good sense of Jim Thorpe's life-style even if he spent little time there. It was plain and simple, with sturdy, solid furniture. Few action films remained to show him performing at his athletic peak, and none were in the home, but a football opponent once described tackling him as "like hitting an oak tree which was doing the hundred in under ten seconds."

Jim's retirement from sports coincided with the arrival of the Great Depression and he often had a hard time finding work. In Los Angeles he toiled as a painter, then began landing low-paying jobs as a movie extra. He was usually in the backgound as an Indian chief or an athlete in B movies, but occasionally showed up in better pictures.

In 1953, two years after a sanitized film biography—*Jim Thorpe, All-American*—was released, Jim died of a heart attack in California. His third wife, Patricia, made an unusual decision about the disposal of his remains. While Jim's body lay in a temporary crypt, she went to Mauch Chunk, Pennsylvania, with a proposition. If the town would change its name to Jim Thorpe, Pennsylvania, she would move his body there and have a memorial constructed. Even though Jim Thorpe had no connection with Mauch Chunk and had probably been unaware of its existence, the economically depressed little town agreed. Jim's body remains there today.

This would be little more than an odd ending to an unusual life, but Sac and Fox tradition makes it more unsettling. Jim's children opposed Patricia Thorpe's plan and continue to do so, insisting that his remains must be returned to their origin and be given a traditional Indian burial. Until this happens, they believe his soul is destined to wander in death much as Jim Thorpe did in his star-crossed life.

A few miles north of Yale I picked up the Cimarron Turnpike and drove west. I stopped at a toll booth sitting in the middle of nothing, maybe ten miles north of Stillwater, home of Oklahoma State University. A pretty woman wearing a Stetson took my money.

"Can I have a receipt?"

"I don't know if I should give you one or not."

"Why?"

"This is Cowboy country." She had seen my SOONER tags as I drove up.

At midafternoon there was very little traffic on the Cimarron Turnpike. The flat prairie was almost treeless and visibility seemed to run forever. Toward the western horizon, the sky had turned dark and ugly, with flashes of lightning zig-zagging downward. I was in bright sunshine and seemed to be driving from daylight into midnight. The light had an eerie quality and made the few trees glow with the half-dark, half-light sky behind them. I turned on the car radio for a weather report. Every lightning flash sent a loud crash of static through the speakers.

Worried about the weather, I took Interstate 35 north instead of staying on smaller highways. My goal for the evening was Wichita, Kansas, to see the Texas League Wranglers play. Kansas was a little far north for a Southern trip, even by my liberal delineation of the South's boundaries. Wichita was in the Texas League, however, and I wanted to see Lawrence-Dumont Stadium. Built in 1934, it was one of the oldest still in use by professional baseball.

In Oklahoma, I had the feeling of being on the edge of a third subregion of the South. First the busy Southeast had given way to the languid Deep South, and now Tex Mex food had replaced grits and dumplings, and cowboy boots and Stetsons were *de rigueur*. There were deeper, more abstract subcultural variations, of course.

I had been in the South for almost three months, and my training as a sociologist dictated that I look for patterns, themes, and motifs. I had expected, before beginning the trip, to collect impressions, categorize them, and sort out the central meaning, but it wasn't happening. W. E. B. DuBois had warned against even trying what he called "car window sociology." Writing in *Souls of Black Folks*, he commented derisively on those who "seek to understand and know the South by devoting the few hours of a holiday trip to un-ravelling the snarl of centuries."

The South had always inspired feeling and handled reason harshly. I had at times felt a part of it, but the snarl of centuries had not unraveled into orderly piles as I looked out the car window.

joined the navy and spent three years playing baseball in Norman, Oklahoma. A high-level team was developed there, including several major league and AA players. Joe's assessment was that it was the second-best navy baseball team in existence during the wartime period. Lieutenant Charlie Gelbert, a shortstop with nine years solid major league experience, ran the team.

"I learned more baseball there than in any other stretch," Joe remembered. "I was better off than working my way up through the minors."

"How did you hit against the major leaguers you faced while you were on the navy team?"

Joe thought for a moment, trying to envision long ago at bats. "I don't remember having any trouble hitting them," he answered.

After the war, Joe was still under contract to the Little Rock Travelers. Little Rock farmed him out to Amarillo in the class C West Texas-New Mexico League for the 1946 season, and Joe's navy apprenticeship began to pay off. He hit .301 and led the league with forty-eight home runs. Next season at Amarillo, Joe formed a fearsome one-two punch with Bob Crues. Hitting right-handed, Crues hit fifty-two home runs while Joe, from the opposite side, contributed thirty-eight. Balls flew through the southwest air in those days; Bill Serena of Lubbock hit fifty-seven home runs that year and kept both Crues and Joe Bauman out of any top offensive categories. In 1948, after Joe left Amarillo, Crues tied the organized baseball record of sixty-nine home runs in one season to give his former teammate something to aim for.

In 1947, Boston paid $10,000 for Joe's contract for their AA Milwaukee team, who in turn farmed him out to Hartford, in the class A Eastern League. Away from the Southwest and playing irregularly, Joe had a subpar season. Ray Sanders, the Boston Braves' first baseman, was at Hartford on a rehabilitation assignment much of the season and Joe alternated with him at first base, accruing only 276 at bats and hitting .275. "Sanders would play if he felt like it," Joe said, "and if he didn't I would be in the lineup."

After the season, the Braves' farm director offered Joe a cut of $200 per month less than he had made the season before. Joe balked, and in the days before Curt Flood challenged the reserve clause, was left with only two options. He could play ball for less than what he thought he was worth, or get out. There was no arbitration and no effective way to negotiate.

"Put me on the voluntary whatever-you-want-to list," Joe told him. "I could make more selling shoe-strings on the corner."

From 1949 through 1951, Joe was out of organized baseball for the second time since his playing days started. He became co-owner of a service station on Route 66 in Oklahoma City, and landed a part-time baseball job in Elk City with a semiprofessional team. The team paid more than the Braves had, and Joe didn't have to work, just play three or four games a week in the western Oklahoma town. In 1949, Joe refused a contract to play with the Southern Association (AA) Atlanta Crackers because he had given the Elk City manager his word that he would finish the season.

If Joe's first four years away from professional baseball during the war had been either beneficial or at least benign, the years from 1949 through 1951 were pivotal in a negative sense. Joe spent his late twenties playing a reduced schedule at a less than professional level. These are typically the "big" years for offensive players, who by then have experience and maturity but still possess sufficient drive, stamina, and reflexive quickness to make their marks. Joe's independence cost him, though how much will never be known.

"In hindsight, I made a mistake but I'm not resentful. It's just that if I had it to do over, I would have taken what they offered to see how far I could go in baseball."

Boston called again and wanted Joe to play the 1952 season for the Atlanta Crackers, but he had made another important contact by then. A doctor whose name Joe no longer remembered, then somehow affiliated with Artesia in the class C Longhorn League, offered to buy Joe's contract from Boston and bring him down to play baseball in New Mexico. Joe agreed, saying, "Okay, but if they charge you more than a jock strap, you're getting took." They struck a deal whereby Joe could buy back his contract for $200 if he didn't like Artesia, and Joe Bauman was back in organized baseball.

In four full Longhorn League seasons, Joe hit home run totals of fifty, fifty-three, seventy-two, and forty-six. His combined batting average over that period was .371, and he averaged 164 runs batted in per season. In his record-setting 1954 season of seventy-two home runs, Joe had 456 total bases in 498 at bats for an all-time high slugging average of .916. Babe Ruth's best was .847.

"How was your fielding?" I joked.

Joe answered seriously, after considering the question as he habitually did. "I would say that I was an above average first baseman."

On his travels through the Longhorn League cities, Joe fell in love with Roswell, New Mexico. He loved the big skies and the clear air and the fact that you could see forever across the desert. "There are no chiggers on the desert," he told me. "That in itself would be enough reason to move here." After the 1953 season, Joe exercised his option and bought back his contract so he could move upstate and play for the Roswell Rockets. He became a community fixture, opening Joe Bauman's Texaco Service and hitting the ball farther and oftener than ever. Roswell was then an independent team, financed by the city.

"We only had fifteen or sixteen guys on the roster. The team bus had six bunks built in the back, a double bunk across the back and two down the sides at the back."

"Who got the bunks?" I asked.

"The five oldest guys and the next day's starting pitcher."

There was no radio coverage for the team, but New Mexico newspapers reported each game. Attendance in the low minors was drying up during that period, and all the home run records were like the bright flare of a roman candle just before it burns itself out. Artesia drew 42,972 in 1952, and in 1953 Joe played before 40,042 home fans. When the Longhorn League was reclassified as a C league, attendance picked up a little. Roswell drew 53,280 for Joe's big year, but slipped to 39,911 in 1955. In his last year, which ended on June 8 because of an ankle injury, Roswell drew only 18,367 even though it had shifted to the higher level class B Southwestern League.

"I played before television, during, and after it became popular, and the crowds were different. Not just in size, which went way down, but in their interest in baseball."

Joe's own declining interest in baseball seemed to parallel that of the minors in general.

"I tried to retire after that 1954 season," Joe said, "but a bunch of the town's businessmen talked me into coming back."

"WHAT? You hit seventy-two home runs and wanted to retire?"

Joe grinned at my surprise. "What was I going to do? Come back and try to hit eighty home runs? Ernie, I had found the town I wanted to live in the rest of my life, I had a good business going and by then I had fallen out of love with baseball. The San Francisco Giants invited me to spring training after the '54 season but I didn't go. I had been playing to get out of baseball that year, not to start something new in it. And I couldn't leave my business all summer. I wouldn't have had a monkey wrench to come back to."

Playing against his wishes in 1955, Joe's offensive output declined. Nonetheless, he hit forty-six home runs and .336. The following winter, Joe stepped out on an icy porch and felt something twist in his ankle. By spring, it continued to hurt when he ran. Not long into the season, X rays showed bone chips floating around. He finally had a legitimate excuse to quit without letting the townsfolk down. Hitting off a bad ankle, Joe had seventeen home runs that year in just 167 at bats. He still managed to hit a home run in about every ten times at bat.

Around noon, we decided it was time to start looking for lunch and Joe offered to drive by the ballpark. It was just south of town, next to the rodeo grounds. Printed sources usually used the name Park Field, but Joe called it Fair Park Field. Before baseball it had been a park for town fairs.

The park was much altered. Right field was still 329 feet from home plate, but the ten-foot-high painted wooden fence had been replaced with easier to maintain chain link all round. The clubhouses and central grandstand were gone, and the wind blew through the grounds unimpeded, trapping sagebrush against the fence.

Until September 1, 1954, Joe Bauman's big season had attracted little national attention even though he had sixty-four home runs. That night, however, 524 fans saw him hit four home runs and a double as Roswell beat Sweetwater, 15–9. With a week left in the

221

regular season, the record of sixty-nine home runs set by Joe Hauser in 1933 and tied by Bob Crues in Amarillo in 1948 was within reach, and the Associated Press picked up the story.

Next evening, Rocket manager Pat Stasey put Joe into the lead-off slot to get him more at bats. Joe had two doubles and a single, but didn't hit one out. The playing manager Stasey, who had put himself into the cleanup slot, had three home runs.

On September 3, photographers from *Life* and *Sports Illustrated* joined local coverage and shot away every time Joe came up to bat. In the bottom of the eighth, with Midland and Roswell tied 4–4, Joe lifted number sixty-nine over the right field wall and beat Midland 7–4.

According to Joe, the eight-team league consisting of Roswell, Artesia, and Carlsbad in New Mexico and Big Spring, Midland, Odessa, San Angelo, and Sweetwater in Texas, had only one band-box ballpark, and that was in Big Spring. The oddly arranged schedule had them playing the next two games in Big Spring before finishing the regular season at Artesia. They bussed over with the press in tow, waiting for Joe to break the record.

Joe never got a chance to break the record in Big Spring; they pitched around him. Even hometown Big Spring fans booed as he drew walk after walk in situations where they should have been pitching to him. On Sunday, September 5, the season ended in Artesia with a doubleheader, and Joe's last chance to break the record came down to one day. Before the game, Artesia NuMexer manager Pat Adair came over to talk to Joe. "I heard what happened in Big Spring. We're gonna pitch to you here. Whatever happens, we aren't going to walk you."

Artesia had an odd-shaped old ballpark with the longest distance running directly down the right field foul line at 360 feet. Also bad for Joe's uppercut swing was the fact that the wind was blowing in from right. In the first inning of the first game, NuMexer pitcher Jose Galardo threw Joe a fast ball and he hit it through the wind and over the tin fence to set a new season home run record for organized baseball. In the second game Joe hit two more home runs, one off Jose Galardo's uncle Frank, just in case the Galardo family didn't feel bad enough already. Artesia, who finished on top of the league with ninety-two wins that season, was overwhelmed 17–0 in the nightcap, succumbing to the fanfare and Roswell's unstoppable hitting magic.

The bat Joe used to hit number seventy went on a traveling bat show and is now in Louisville at the Hillerich and Bradsby plant. They gave him a black bat with gold engraving in exchange.

"I didn't make any real money from the record," Joe said. "Lot of ham, though. We got a free ham that year for every home run we hit."

Joe knew a small cantina on a quiet street in Roswell, and we went there for lunch. Over green chili enchiladas and *Carta Blanca* beer, I asked him how he did it.

"Hell, I don't know how I did it. I didn't have a slump all season, but I don't know why. Ernie, the ball looked that big all year." Joe made a circle the size of a canteloupe with his large hands.

"That last big doubleheader gave you a .400 batting average for the year. Were you aware of that at the time?"

He sat for a moment, trying to put the day together in his mind, and finally said simply, "That was secondary."

The sky was on fire in Artesia. Refineries were everywhere, and flames shot out of pipes that pierced the sky with unending burnoff. I had stopped to see the ballpark in Artesia after leaving Roswell, and it was still just as Joe had described it. The eccentric configuration had straightaway center field at 355 feet, while the right field foul line was 360 feet away, and the left field power alley measured in the 340s. The fences were still covered in tin, and the wind was blowing in from right field. In a direct line from home, over second base, beyond dead center, a pipe several blocks away extended up about fifty feet, and an orange flame licked the perfect blue of the sky.

no room to work, and had to build Farm Road 170 up the slope of a crag at a fifteen-degree grade.

After driving through Presidio and turning north toward Marfa, I passed through two blockades set up by the border patrol to intercept illegal aliens. This made a total of four I'd seen since entering the Big Bend country. The officers were very interested in Sweetspot, as the back looked like an ideal hiding place. When they discovered it was set up for more mundane purposes, they asked about my trip in a friendly way, and we talked awhile. This was lonely country.

Driving several hundred miles through the Big Bend country, the sight of other cars had been so infrequent that occupants invariably waved, probably more so because I was driving the local vehicle of choice, a pickup. This had quickly become habitual, and driving west on US 90 I tossed out three unanswered waves before the habit was broken.

At Van Horn, Texas, US 90 ended at Interstate 10. I intended to take the interstate northwest only a short distance, then cut through one of the emptiest, most desolate corners of west Texas and stay the night at Hueco Tanks State Park, thirty miles west of El Paso. The plan was fine, but before leaving Van Horn, I made a Texas-sized mistake.

Maybe the Texas sun had penetrated my Nashville cowboy hat and baked my brain. More likely, it was three months of watching hundreds of batters swing at thousands of pitches, and not ever feeling the sensations myself. At any rate, a combination baseball-golf driving range appeared roadside and some force I couldn't control pulled Sweetspot into a parking place. I walked over to a batting cage with a fistful of quarters.

The balls were hard rubber, and had been pounded into misshapen masses only vaguely resembling spheroids. I set the machine on what I thought was a hittable seventy miles per hour and took a few warmup swings. The balls thumped out of the mechanical arm at what seemed at first to be blinding speed, and because of the weird shapes, they did unpredictable things. They sailed in, broke away, and even at a constant speed, kept me offstride. After four or five swings my timing improved and finally I met one with that contact that seems to move the bat through the ball with only a slight, satisfying resistance. The ball was lined solidly out into the dry rocky field and I coiled to do it again, to send the next one even farther. The pitch came in and lurched impossibly up and away, and before my jerky follow-through was completed I felt a stabbing pain in my lower back. The slightest additional movements caused spasms to shoot through my torn back muscles, and I racked the aluminum bat, limped carefully back to the truck, and painfully lifted myself into the cab. Batting practice was over.

Half an hour up the interstate at Sierra Blanca I turned north on a rough-looking ranch road. Almost fifty miles lay between Sierra Blanca and another principal highway to the north. The road was paved except for a few stretches, but in parts the paving was in bad repair, and even in the smooth-riding pickup, the bumps transmitted a sharp message to my damaged back muscles. About halfway along the back road, sweating profusely, I stopped.

I put a lawn chair in the shade beside the truck, took a few aspirin, fashioned an ice pack from a plastic bag, and wedged it between my back and the chair canvas. Even in late afternoon, the sun was fierce and I had to refill the ice bag within twenty minutes. To the west I could see a prominent peak, the Sierra Blanca, at about seven thousand feet and to the east, Dome Peak, a few thousand feet lower. The only moving things I could see were hawks, soaring on air drafts far above the high desert floor.

Sitting on my third ice pack, a startling thought occurred to me: I didn't really have to go to El Paso! I could take County Road 1111 back to Sierra Blanca, ease onto the interstate, and by the time of tomorrow evening's game between the El Paso Diablos and the Midland Angels, a good chunk of the drive home would be behind me. I had been to El Paso once before, so it wasn't as if I would miss seeing a new city. More immediately, County Road 1111 looked like a washboard, and the muscle spasms in my back had worn away most of my energy.

On the other hand, El Paso had been the mark from the start. "Going all the way to El Paso," I had been telling people all across the South. El Paso wasn't just one more ball game and one more city, it was, as the psychologists say, closure. It was the most distant

233

western point where you could still make the case that you were in the South.

I hadn't put words to it, but had been feeling a strange combination of gladness and gloom ever since arriving in Texas. It wasn't because Texans hated my SOONERS license plate, but because the trip was almost over. I wanted to be home, to see my wife, pick up my life, and write about fresh, vivid memories. But the road was bewitching. For months, every day had provided choices that depended on me alone, and the incredibly limp and tattered Rand McNally atlas on the front seat had provided the means. Going home meant trading a steering wheel for a desk. I didn't even have a job anymore, and that would require some adjustment. I would have to do things I wasn't looking forward to, such as selling Sweetspot to help pay for the trip. The old truck had been in the family for more than two decades, and had been so reliable and trustworthy that I no longer gave a thought to being stranded, even stopped in the middle of the desert. Poor reward, to take her home and sell her.

"You should know when to give it up," the logical side of my brain said. "Could be a good game tomorrow," said the other side. The questions I had begun the trip with had by now been answered. I had wondered whether the Old South of myth and lore was still there, or its regional subculture had gone with the winds of the twentieth century. After three months, I was sure that the traditional values and rules of the South lay quietly but strongly throughout the vast territory. The symbols of southern tradition were under attack, but counterattacks were in evidence everywhere. Writers like humorist Lewis Grizzard, a defender of the folkways of the traditional southern white male, were selling well across Dixie. Advertising for impersonal fast food chains had been regionalized, offering "skat-through" service. When the state of Alabama lowered the Confederate flag from state property, opinion in Georgia and Mississippi favoring keeping the stars and bars seemed to become more entrenched.

Even the mesmerizing southern speech held sway except in larger urban centers or increasingly popular sun belt retirement areas, penetrated *en masse* by Yankee refugees. Early in the trip, before I became accustomed to different, slower cadences, I had failed to understand that "bald" peanuts had been cooked by boiling, that a "born" baseball game was one the speaker found boring, or that a suggestion to take the road to "your right" did not mean going to the village of Yorerot. The South may no longer be a monolithic regional subculture, but the old ways are visible to anyone who drives the less-traveled roads.

The other question had to do with changes in minor league baseball. I had predicted that the southern minor leagues would remain true to the classic baseball formula of diehard fans and gritty, straightforward, all-or-nothing baseball. I had been wrong. Southern minor league baseball had evolved into a new form of entertainment. The obsessed fans, like the gentleman in Chattanooga who shouted instructions to players over a megaphone, were still there in small numbers, but a club that opened its doors today with no promotions or giveaways would attract only a handful of these relics and no others. I had found southern minor league baseball to be different from the old days, but with an appeal and charm that still reflected the simplicity and purity missing from the big league game. In Columbia, South Carolina, I had seen the dugout empty, not to engage in a tedious, irrelevant brawl with opponents, but to watch a young boy tap dance on the dugout roof. In Asheville, North Carolina, I watched two young boys' eyes grow wide with wonder when the Spartanburg manager slipped them used baseball equipment. In Little Rock, I had noted that players approached autograph signing as a privilege, and smiled as they signed their names. My attendance at ninety games had not resulted in disappointment at failure to find the experiences of my youth, but in a slow conversion. I had felt safe, comfortable, secure, and happy in the South's minor league parks, and didn't regret a mile of the summer's journey. Besides, I had been right on 50 percent of my pretrip predictions, and a .500 batting average was nothing to be ashamed of for a season.

I climbed slowly into the pickup cab and started the engine. Out of habit, I looked into the rearview mirror, though I had been sitting there for over two hours and not a single vehicle had passed. County Road 1111 was really too narrow for turning around any-

The umpire's clenched fist was the first acknowledgment, and then six thousand fans were on their feet. They may have come for the promotions or because they had free tickets, but at that moment they were baseball fans, and they were applauding a professional. He ran in, head down, no emotion showing, and disappeared into the dugout.

I checked the media guide later. The player who had made that eloquent catch might as well have been wearing NP, no prospect, for a uniform number. He was twenty-six, already old by minor league standards, and had never played higher than AA ball. He had spent the last three years shuffling between the parent club's class A and AA teams. The game hadn't been on the line, the percentage play was off the wall for a double. Why, then, this strange gift?

I tried to remember my youthful experiences with baseball as movement, with the exhilaration involved in arresting the flight of a bright white sphere, or driving it out in a different direction with a bat. I thought of the relaxed feeling that grew with a game of catch, the rocking, rythmic use of large body muscles, and I recalled the pump of energy that fueled a headlong sprint to first base. Those joys had been learned before baseball meant status, required dedication, or entailed commitment. They were the pleasures of baseball as play. And my sore back was evidence that the years hadn't veiled those senses, no more than they had in the flying Midlands' left fielder.

Beneath baseball as business, as pageantry, or even as nostalgia, there is that irreducible essence. It is beyond reason but is sensed by the multitudes, whether they perform the act or spontaneously rise to applaud in its presence. A young Willie Mays, asked to analyze the meaning of baseball, put it in words once: "They pitch it, I hit it. They hit it, I catch it."

A half moon hung over the Franklin Mountains as I left the ballpark. The mountains looked dark against the deep purple sky, like a crudely cut first grade art project, jagged black construction paper tacked to a purple backdrop, and over everything a yellow cutout moon, which was far too bright and shiny to be real.

Suggestions for Further Reading

Each of the following books contains descriptive or statistical material on baseball in the South:

Benson, Michael. *Ballparks of North America: A Comprehensive Historical Reference to Baseball Grounds, Yards and Stadiums, 1845 to Present.* Jefferson, NC: McFarland & Company, Inc., 1989.

Blake, Mike. *The Minor Leagues: A Celebration of the Little Show.* New York: Wynwood Press, 1991.

Brooks, Ken. *The Last Rebel Yell: Baseball's Forgotten Alabama-Florida League.* Lynn Haven, FL: Seneca Publishing, 1986.

Johnson, Lloyd, and Miles Wolff (eds.). *The Encyclopedia of Minor League Baseball.* Durham, NC: Baseball America, Inc., 1993.

Lamb, David. *Stolen Season: A Journey through America and Baseball's Minor Leagues.* New York: Random House, 1991.

O'Neal, Bill. *The Texas League: A Century of Baseball 1888–1987.* Austin, TX: Eakin Press, 1987.

O'Neal, Bill. *The Southern League: Baseball in Dixie 1885–1994.* Austin, TX: Eakin Press, 1994.

Sullivan, Neil J. *The Minors.* New York: St. Martin's Press, 1990.

Southern Minor League Baseball Clubs

TEAM	LOCATION	PARK	SEATS
Florida State League (A)			
(West)			
Charlotte Rangers	Pt. Charlotte, FL	Charlotte County	6,026
Clearwater Phillies	Clearwater, FL	Jack Russell	7,384
Dunedin Blue Jays	Dunedin, FL	Dunedin	6,214
Fort Meyers Miracle	Ft. Meyers, FL	Lee County Sports	7,500
St. Petersburg Cards	St. Petersburg, FL	Al Lang	7,004
Sarasota White Sox	Sarasota, FL	Ed Smith	7,500
(East)			
Daytona Cubs	Daytona Beach, FL	Jackie Robinson	4,900
Ft. Lauderdale Red Sox	Ft. Lauderdale, FL	Ft. Lauderdale Sta.	8,300
Lakeland Tigers	Lakeland, FL	Joker Marchant	7,000
Osceola Astros	Kissimmee, FL	Osceola County	5,100
St. Lucie Mets	St. Lucie, FL	Thomas J. White	7,400
Vero Beach Dodgers	Vero Beach, FL	Holman	6,474
West Palm Beach Expos	West Palm Beach FL	Municipal	4,400
South Atlantic League (A)			
(North)			
Asheville Tourists	Asheville, NC	McCormick Field	3,500
Charleston Sternwheelers	Charleston, WV	Watt Powell Park	6,000

Index

About the Author

ERNEST J. GREEN was a professor of sociology until 1993. After returning from his trip through the South, he said goodbye to academia and officially retired. Since completing *The Diamonds of Dixie*, Green has been writing his next book, a history of the Chesapeake and Ohio Canal. He has contributed baseball articles and reviews to several publications, including *Nine* and *The Encyclopedia of United States Popular Culture*.